LOST BILOXI

LOST BILOXI

EDMOND BOUDREAUX

Published by The History Press
Charleston, SC 29403
www.historypress.net

Front cover: Biloxi City Hall. *Courtesy of the Alan Santa Cruz Collection.*
Back cover, top: White House Hotel. *Courtesy of the Alan Santa Cruz Collection.*
Back cover, bottom: Biloxi Town Green. *Author's collection.*

First published 2015

ISBN 978.1.5402.0290.1

Library of Congress Control Number: 2015943181

Contents

Acknowledgements 7
Introduction 9

1. Bailey House 11
2. Brielmaier and Foretich Houses 16
3. Creole Cottage 21
4. Dantzler House 26
5. Father Ryan House 31
6. Fisherman's Cottage 38
7. Pleasant Reed House 41
8. Old Mud Daub House: Biloxi's Oldest Home 47
9. Old Brick House 51
10. Old Spanish House 56
11. Gunston Hall/White Pillars 60
12. Tullis-Toledano Manor and the Manor Families 69
13. Palmer House 76
14. Edgewater Gulf Hotel 80
15. Avelez Hotel 86
16. Tivoli Hotel 91
17. White House Hotel 96
18. Magnolia Hotel: Queen of the Watering Holes 103
19. Baricev's Seafood Harbor Restaurant and Lounge 109
20. Gus Stevens Restaurant and Supper Club 113

21. Friendship House Restaurant 120
22. Baldwin Wood Lighthouse 127
23. Biloxi's USO and Community Center 136
24. Biloxi's City Hall and Market 141
25. Pizzati Pavilion and the L&N Park 146
26. Point Cadet Plaza and the Maritime and Seafood Industry Museum 150
27. Eight Flags 156

Bibliography 163
Index 169
About the Author 173

Acknowledgements

While I have put many years of research into this book, certain people have helped make this book possible. This includes a special group of local historians who influenced me. They are: Julia Cook Guice, Mary Louise Adkinson, Murella Hebert Powell, Kat Bergeron and Dr. Val Husley.

In 1985, I became involved with the Maritime and Seafood Industry Museum located in Biloxi. It developed into a first-class museum, but in 2005, Hurricane Katrina destroyed the building and all the exhibits less than one year after a total remodeling of and addition to the museum. Today, it is located in a new building. The museum's records, documents and pictures played a big part in the research for this book. Thank-you to Alan Santa Cruz and Lynn and Sandra Paterson, who allowed their collection of Gulf Coast postcards to become an important part of this book. Thank-you to Bettie Fore for allowing her White family photographs to become an important part of Chapter 17.

The local history and genealogy department of the Harrison County Library System also deserves special thanks.

I would also like to thank The History Press for recognizing Biloxi's lost and forgotten history through the printing of this book.

Last but not least, I have a very special appreciation for my wife, Virginia, who edited my work and kept me straight.

Introduction

Lost Biloxi is a collection of stories of historic structures and iconic businesses that made Biloxi a historic city. Each chapter covers a structure lost to hurricanes or lost in time. Each structure had ties to the people who lived in them, the citizens of Biloxi and Biloxi's past. Some of the historical structures are the Old Brick House, the Old Spanish House, the Baldwin Wood Lighthouse, the Biloxi City Hall and Market, Gus Stevens Restaurant and Supper Club, Six Gun Junction and the Edgewater Gulf Hotel.

Hurricanes Camille (1969) and Katrina (2005) destroyed historical structures that had become part of the fabric of our lives in Biloxi. Some of these lost structures were the Bailey House, the Father Ryan House, the Tullis-Toledano Manor, the Foretich House, the Brielmaier House and the Dantzler House. Many more were reduced to piles of wood and brick. Before Katrina, there were 160 historical structures listed on the National or Mississippi Register of Historic Places, as well the other structures from the City of Biloxi register of historical structures. Of those historical landmark structures, 60 were lost in Katrina. A few suffered extreme damage but survived. In some cases, historical structures were lost to modern progress, or their histories were forgotten in time. This book is a collection of the history and photographs of some of these structures.

1

Bailey House

Most locals know the Bailey House only as the old Holy Angels Nursery. Holy Angels Nursery operated from 1942 until the 1990s. Many generations of locals were taken care of by the nuns at nursery and/or attended its kindergarten. The Bailey House has also been referred to as the Wesley House. The house was constructed between 1846 and 1852 and was on the National Register of Historical Places. Over the years, the structure fell into a state of disrepair and would have needed a complete overhaul to restore it to its former beauty. In 2005, its new owners were considering whether it could be restored or possibly torn down and replaced with a modern structure or a parking lot. Yes, it was on the National Register of Historical Places, and most people believe that, because of this, it was protected. The truth was, because of its condition, it could have been condemned. At that point, a structure can be removed from the register.

The Bailey House was the oldest structure on Point Cadet and was Biloxi's only early two-story frame house located on the beach. It was located at 204 Beach Boulevard on the corner of Cedar Street and Beach Boulevard.

In the mid-1800s, a subdivision known as Summerville was selling lots on Point Cadet. Nathan Evans Bailey, a vinegar manufacturer from New Orleans, purchased two lots in the Summerville subdivision. The second lot was purchased in 1846, and by 1852, the Baileys had moved from New Orleans to Biloxi. On May 7, 1896, Bailey filed a will in Harrison County leaving all real and personal property to his youngest daughter, Ada C. Bailey. He also listed Nathan E. Bailey as his youngest son. On

The Wesley House, sponsored by the missionary board of the Methodist Episcopal Church South. *Courtesy of the Maritime and Seafood Industry Museum.*

February 2, 1902, Nathan Bailey died at eighty-eight years of age and was buried in the Biloxi Cemetery. There were some indications that the home was sold in 1901, before his death, to Angeline L. Bailey Dolbear, his eldest daughter. Bailey's daughter Ada continued to live in Biloxi until her death in 1924.

Over time, a series of events changed the course of history for the Bailey House. Reverend T.L. Melien of New Orleans headed the Methodist Episcopal Church South's Seashore District. Sometime before 1907, Reverend Melien made a request for more ministries along the Gulf Coast. In 1907, the Woman's Board of Home Missions hired and sent Minnie Boykin to work among the seafood industry workers. In Biloxi, Boykin rented a cottage on the corner of Howard Avenue and Oak Street. She successfully recruited volunteers, organized a home missionary society and began her social and religious work. The mission mainly targeted the Bohemians and other immigrant workers. Boykin personally visited any seafood workers' home that would have her.

In 1909, the missionary board of the Methodist Episcopal Church South leased the Bailey House, but its doors did not open until October 1910. The mission soon referred to the home as the Wesley House. The Wesley House offered evening school classes for the children and adults who worked in the factories. Sewing and homemaker classes were offered to girls between six and sixteen. In the evenings, there were social games, music and singing for the children. A boys' club and a mothers' club were started. Of course, there were also the Sunday school classes and religious services.

In addition to the other activities, a daily kindergarten class and nursery was set up. The day nursery was open from 7:00 a.m. to 5:00 p.m. and served two to three meals per day for five cents per day. When the children were old enough for kindergarten, they would attend from 9:00 a.m. to 11:30 a.m. for free.

In the early 1900s, Bishop Gunn, the bishop of the Catholic Dioceses of Natchez, noted that the Catholic families' spiritual and physical needs were not being cared for by the Mother Church. He urged Father Alphonse Ketels, the pastor of the Nativity of the Blessed Virgin Mary (BVM) Church of Biloxi, to open a mission church and a school taught

The St. Michael Catholic Church's Holy Angels Nursery, also known as the Bailey House. *Author's collection.*

by the Sisters of Mercy. In 1907, the St. Michael the Archangel Mission was opened on Point Cadet. Then in 1913, Sisters of Mercy M. Mildred Hart and Dorothea Crahen began teaching in the first St. Michael school. By 1917, St. Michael had become a parish, and the school was growing. In 1939, St. Michael Parish had eight Sisters of Mercy living in the parish convent. One of these sisters was Sister Mary Adrienne Curet, whose life touched many locals. During this period, the Bailey House continued as a Methodist mission until 1940.

In 1942, the property was purchased by St. Michael's Church and held in trust by the Catholic Diocese of Natchez. The Sisters of Mercy began to operate the house as the Methodist ladies had, as a nursery and kindergarten. It was renamed Holy Angels Nursery, and by 1949, Sister Mary Adrienne was listed as sister superior. Sister Adrienne became the mainstay of Holy Angels Nursery. Many generations of locals were cared for and taught by these Sisters of Mercy.

The Bailey House has weathered numerous hurricanes, but Hurricane Camille, in 1969, was one of its biggest tests. As the storm approached the

The casino barge resting on Holy Angels Nursery. *Author's collection.*

Mississippi Gulf Coast, the Sisters of Mercy knew they would have to leave Holy Angels. Before their departure, Sister Adrienne buried a small statue of St. Joseph at the front steps. She prayed to St. Joseph to protect the house because mothers from storm-damaged homes would need a place to leave small children so they could clean up. Anyone who was present for the aftermath of Hurricane Camille will tell you the Gulf Coast looked like a war zone. Yet the Bailey House was untouched, with only storm debris washed up to the steps where the St. Joseph statute was buried. Sister Adrienne continued at Holy Angels until poor health forced her to retire to Vicksburg. Holy Angels continued as a nursery and kindergarten until the 1990s.

As Hurricane Katrina approached the Mississippi Gulf Coast, no statue of St. Joseph was buried near the Bailey House steps. Everyone assumed that Katrina would be like so many other past storms but not as severe as Camille. The Bailey House, like numerous historical structures, was reduced to a pile of debris and lost for this and future generations.

2

Brielmaier and Foretich Houses

Two to three weeks after Hurricane Katrina, I found myself working on Water Street between Main and Lameuse Streets. The debris was piled high around the buildings with parts of Water Street still blocked. As I worked, I noticed a shiny object near the debris-covered sidewalk. As I lifted the object, I realized that it was a battered Main Street Christmas ornament. Ironically, the ornament depicted the Brielmaier House that had stood on Biloxi Town Green. It was from a shipment of new ornaments that Main Street had received just before Katrina came ashore. The ornaments were replicas of the Dantzler House, the Brielmaier House and other historical structures. They had been stored in the Brielmaier and Foretich Houses. As Katrina assaulted the town green, these replicas—like their real-life counterparts—were pounded and destroyed by Katrina.

The Brielmaier House was built about 1895 and was originally located at 436 Main Street. Paul W. Brielmaier worked for the T.J. Roselle Sash and Blind Factory and was married to Minnie Swetman. Minnie was the sister of Orcenith George, J.W. Swetman and Mrs. Henry "Tootie" Graves. J.W. was one of the founders of the Peoples Bank in 1896, and Orcenith joined the bank in 1903. The property originally belonged to Mrs. Graves, who sold it to Paul and Minnie. Paul and Minnie lived with Mrs. Graves on Main Street while their home was constructed. Each day, Paul would return from work, and he and Minnie would cross Main Street and work on their home late into the night. Paul and Minnie constructed a three-room structure shaped like a T with a gallery around the front room.

The Brielmaier House on Biloxi Town Green. *Courtesy of the Maritime and Seafood Industry Museum.*

The work was completed about 1895, and the Brielmaiers moved into their new home. Paul created some of the fanciest Victorian detailing found along the Mississippi Gulf Coast. It's not known if the detailing was completed before the Brielmaier family moved into the home or after. Paul appears to have been quite talented with carving tools. The latticework that adorned the porch was magnificent. Each bedroom had identical mantels with Ionic pilasters on each side of the fireplace. But Paul did not stop there—the windows, doors, trim and baseboards were all very ornate.

Sometime between 1904 and 1905, Paul began construction on the John E. Swetman home, which survived Hurricane Katrina and is located at 567 Howard Avenue. Paul was the foreman at the T.J. Roselle Sash and Blind Factory but found time to build the Swetman house with magnificent detailing. John E. Swetman was listed as the owner of the Central Meat Market in the 1905 Biloxi City Directory. He was involved in numerous enterprises, including a tugboat service that ran between Biloxi and Ship Island. Paul, in time, bought out T.J. Roselle Sash and Blind Factory and renamed it Brielmaier Sash and Blind Factory. Minnie became the bookkeeper and ordering clerk, as well as handling all the banking business. Paul was a gifted craftsman who not only built houses but also added magnificent detailing.

Paul and Minnie had six children—five boys and one girl, Margaret. One of the boys died at about ten months of age. In 1920, an addition was added to the rear of the Brielmaier House.

Paul built a home at 217 Lameuse Street for his son Phillip and family. Phillip; his wife, Ruby; and daughter, Annelle, moved into this home shortly after Phillip's return from World War I. Paul's carpentry skills were that of a master carpenter, a woodcarver and an artisan in his own right.

After Paul's death, Minnie lived well into her nineties. In 1960, at the age of ninety, she stood as matron of honor for her granddaughter, Minnie Jacque Lynn Shimkus.

In the living room of the Brielmaier home was a huge mantel made of cedar and mahogany. The mantel was built by Paul and originally was installed at 444 Main Street, another Brielmaier family home. Two of Paul's sons, Emory B. and Phillip W. Brielmaier, moved the mantel to 436 Main Street before the house at 444 Main Street was torn down. The carved and decorated mantel rose nearly to the ceiling and caught the eye of any visitor to the home.

The Foretich House on Biloxi Town Green. *Courtesy of the Maritime and Seafood Industry Museum.*

The Brielmaier house was listed on the National Register of Historic Places. In 1982, the house was donated to the City of Biloxi. In 1986, it was moved from 436 Main Street to the town Green to become the centerpiece of the visitor center.

The Foretich House was a single shotgun-style home with a lateral wing. The gallery, or porch, wrapped around the home. The structure had a hipped roof with simple rectangular columns. The Foretich House was originally at 134 Delauney Street. The home was built in the late 1800s or early 1900s. Before 1911, the Drake family owned the property and were possibly responsible for its construction. The heirs of the Drake family sold the property to Rosa Bourdon in 1911. After her death in 1942, she left the property to her nieces Ernestine Desporte Thompson and Evelyn Desporte Lancaster. Then in 1949, they sold the property to Leo V. and Lottie Foretich.

The Foretich House was donated to the City of Biloxi, and in 1986, it was moved to the town green. The Foretich House sat behind the Brielmaier House and was joined together by a raised porch and shoofly. A shoofly was a raised platform with rails that wrapped around a tree with a staircase for access. It afforded individuals an excellent view of the Gulf of Mexico. With

The Hurricane Katrina Memorial. *Author's collection.*

the addition of another shoofly around an oak tree west of the two homes, the town green was complete. Over the years, the town green became a place where numerous cultural events, weddings and a wonderful display of Christmas lights during the holidays were held. Hurricane Katrina not only destroyed the Brielmaier and Foretich Houses but also changed the face of the town green. Today, the Hurricane Katrina Memorial sits on the site that was once the Brielmaier and Foretich Houses.

3

Creole Cottage

Creole styled houses have French Louisiana origins. This style of home was the product of colonial development in the eighteenth century. These structures had a gallery, or porch, and a high roof covered the home. They were built this way so cross breezes could keep the homes cool. Most homes of this style had outside entrances to each room, which allowed air to circulate when the exterior doors were opened. The roof was built above the whole structure with the gallery under the roof. They were built as either a two- or five-room structure. In later years, an even number of windows and doors—either two or four—were placed along the main façade.

The Creole Cottage consists of five rooms, with two large rooms in the front, two small rooms behind the large rooms and a small gallery, which had been enclosed, was also considered a room. The structure has four openings in the front and a fireplace with a box mantel that was built in the eighteenth century. This is an influence from New Orleans, where the box mantels were typically used.

The Creole Cottage's history begins much earlier than post Katrina. It is unclear when the structure was built. The Creole Cottage was located at 127 Lameuse Street just south of Jackson Street. Between 1830 and 1840, John Delauney built ten of these Creole-style cottages to rent to tourists who visited the American Riviera of the South, as the Gulf Coast was known. The cottages were used for single or double occupancy during winter or summer tourist seasons. These Creole cottages were built on land purchased by Adele Delauney, John's wife, in 1829. Unfortunately, the marriage didn't

The Creole Cottage, Biloxi's first library. *Author's collection.*

last, and after the divorce, Adele, who then married Arne Bernard, gained possession of the property after legal proceedings. The Bernards sold the property to Pierre Hugonin in 1845. After Hugonin's death, his heirs sold the property to Anthony Castaned during an auction in 1879. The property was described as having two old houses and separate kitchens that were in need of repair. In 1905, after the death of Anthony Castaned, the property was once more on the auction block. This time, Harry T. Howard purchased the property with plans to use it for public good. Howard leased the property to a charitable organization know as Biloxi's King's Daughters for use as a public library.

The King's Daughters began the first public library in Mississippi in 1898 with one hundred books, but in 1900, it was destroyed by a fire. Howard later donated the house and property to the King's Daughters organization. King's Daughters was a worldwide organization with community chapters made up of local ladies who performed charitable services in their communities.

The first indication of an interest in a public library appeared in the *Biloxi Daily Herald* on April 8, 1893. Supporters met to begin the incorporation of the Biloxi Library Association. A second meeting was planned, and the public was invited. The *Herald* reported:

It is to be hoped that all persons who are interested in the moral and intellectual advancement of Biloxi will not fail to be in attendance.

By 1898, the library had been established, and after 1905, it was located in the Creole Cottage. On March 23, 1911, the *Herald* reported that over 1,000 volumes had been loaned. During a period of three months, 1,098 books had been loaned out to the public. At this time, the library had 3,000 books. In addition to the books, a large number of magazines were on hand. The librarian, Millie Rodenberg, reported that the collection included reference books, encyclopedias, histories, poetry, travel guides, fiction books and dictionaries.

Rodenberg was the first librarian hired by the King's Daughters. The group also allowed her to operate a private school in the library as a stipend to her salary. Rodenberg had been a schoolteacher for many years before becoming a librarian. Rodenberg served as the librarian until 1925, when a new library was built. On June 25, 1930, she passed away in Biloxi at the age of eighty-two. The *Herald* reported that most of her life was spent helping educate others. As for being Biloxi's first librarian, the *Herald* indicated that Rodenberg was knowledgeable on many subjects and familiar with all the books in the library.

The back view of the Creole Cottage. *Author's collection.*

One interesting note about the three families mentioned in this chapter: the Howard, Delauney and Rodenberg families all have streets named in their honor. During the 1920s, the population growth in Biloxi was having an effect on all aspects of the city, including the library. The library needed to expand due to the growth in Biloxi's population, as well as book donations. The truth was that it had outgrown the Creole Cottage before 1920. The King's Daughters decided to sell the cottage and use the profits to purchase land for a new library. The corner of Water Street and Lameuse Street was purchased and donated to the city, and by 1925, the new library had been built. The Biloxi Library was at this location until 1977.

In no time at all, the new library grew and was soon packed with books, with little room between stacks. Many individuals who grew up in Biloxi can remember going to this library for school purposes as well as personal enjoyment. For many, it was the only library they had ever known.

During the period from 1925 to 1973, the Creole Cottage was nothing more than a structure in Biloxi's downtown area. The building fell into a state of disrepair, but all that was about to change. The October 24, 1973 *Daily Herald* reported that Dr. Harry J. Schmidt Sr. had donated the Creole Cottage, Biloxi's oldest library, to the city.

The Creole Cottage facing Rue Magnolia. *Author's collection.*

The City of Biloxi decided to move the Creole Cottage to the parking lot of the city's library. Under the direction of architect John Collins, the city's maintenance department moved the structure. Collins also handled the preservation and restoration of the cottage. In addition to those duties, Collins and Glen Swetman of the Peoples Bank were in charge of a fundraising drive to offset the expenses of moving and restoration of the structure. The cottage remained at this location until 1976.

In 1975, the City of Biloxi was planning events for the country's bicentennial. One of the proposed projects was the building of a Bicentennial Plaza and a new Biloxi Library and Cultural Center. Turnbull and Associates of San Francisco designed the complex, and the Holiday Inn Construction Division of Memphis was in charge of construction. The groundbreaking ceremony took place on October 24, 1975. During the construction phase, the Creole Cottage was moved to the plaza and restored.

In September 1977, the Biloxi Library and Cultural Center was formally opened. When it opened, the Creole Cottage was the centerpiece of the Bicentennial Plaza. The cottage was restored as a 1905 library with a schoolroom. It contained historical displays of school and library materials. It continued as a museum until 1982. After that date, it was used by many organizations and was finally used as city office space.

As Hurricane Katrina assaulted Biloxi, surge water surrounded and flooded the Creole Cottage, but it survived. After Katrina, the Creole Cottage was restored and relocated to Rue Magnolia, preserving Biloxi's first library for future generations.

4
Dantzler House

The Biloxi Lighthouse is hard to miss due to its location in the middle of Highway 90, but before Katrina, another structure also caught the eyes of tourists and locals. Many photographers used it as a backdrop for lighthouse shots. This two-storied, picturesque building with wraparound galleries on both floors was the Dantzler House. Hurricane Katrina would turn it into nothing more than a pile of debris. This magnificent building, with its gorgeous cut- and stained-glass windows, was a jewel by itself. It is referred to as the Robinson-Maloney Home by some and listed so in architectural studies.

The Dantzler House was built in 1849 by John Ghamm "J.G." Robinson, an English cotton planter. The four-acre property had sold for $3,300 in 1842. In 1853, the *New Orleans Daily Picayune*, forefather of the *New Orleans Times-Picayune*, had referred to the home as a princely mansion and asserted that no equal along the Gulf Coast existed. The writer of the article was a personal friend of Robinson. He indicated that a few friends and he had boarded one of the New Orleans yachting fleet's favorite yachts. They sailed to Biloxi in no time and tied to the pier of an old revered friend, J.G. Robinson. Robinson had given them a hearty welcome and invited them into his home. The *Daily Picayune* indicated that Robinson had a fondness for sailing and had always enjoyed the manly and gentlemanly sport.

The Robinson home was described as spacious and adorned with engravings, pictures and plates. The galleries were similar to Beauvoir, the historic last home of Jefferson Davis, the president of the Confederacy.

The Dantzler House when the United Service Organization operated a female military personnel facility. *Courtesy of the Alan Santa Cruz Collection.*

The Robinson home galleries extended around three sides of the home. Robinson loved to entertain guests, so his home included a billiard room and a ten-pin bowling alley. He also owned a fleet of yachts, which included the *Sylph*, the *Coquette* and the *Fairy*.

The Robinson property had a large horse stable and kennels for a large variety of dogs. Robinson also owned pigs, which included some imported Berkshire pigs, and poultry, which included gamecocks and a Shanghai rooster.

In 1855, a hurricane hit the Mississippi Gulf Coast, destroying numerous homes, boats, wharfs and bathhouses. It also washed away dirt from the foundation of the Biloxi Light. The Robinson family lost a large wharf and an ornamental bathhouse, and their home and furniture suffered water and wind damage. Robinson had a stone wall along the shoreline that was totally destroyed. Two of his yachts, the *Sylph* and *Coquette*, just happened to be in Biloxi Back Bay and escaped any damage.

Robinson sold the home and property in 1873 to Frederic and Lena Gaupp, natives of France. The Gaupp family did not own the home very long, selling it in 1884. On April 8, 1887, Lena died. Two years later, Frederic died, on August 9, 1889. Both are buried in the Biloxi Cemetery.

Inside the Dantzler House when it was Notre Dame High School. *Courtesy of the Maritime and Seafood Industry Museum.*

The Dr. James M. Maloney family purchased the house from the Gaupp family. The Maloney family began to modernize the home in 1909. They transformed the home from its early Gulf Coast style to the Colonial Revival style that was popular in the early twentieth century. They retained the property until 1912, when it was sold to E.C. Johnston.

About nine years later, Johnston transfered ownership to A.F. Dantzler. Dantzler, a coast lumberman, purchased the building in 1921. His purchase included all of the furnishings in the home at the time of the sale.

In 1943, Dantzler sold the home and property to the Diocese of Natchez-Jackson for use as Notre Dame High School. The all-boy school operated at this location until 1953, when a new school was built and opened on Keegan's Bayou. The diocese then used it from 1953 to 1956 for the all-girl Sacred Heart Academy. Girls who were in the tenth through twelfth grades attended school in the Dantzler House. Then in 1958, the Irish Sisters of Mercy converted it into living quarters and lived there until 1969.

In 1969, Hurricane Camille damaged the structure, but repairs were made. Then in 1970, the City of Biloxi paid $110,000 for the beachfront

Hurricane Katrina reduced the Dantzler House to a pile of wood. *Author's collection.*

The Biloxi Lighthouse Visitor Center on the former Dantzler House site, 2015. *Author's collection.*

lot and building. It was used to replace the USO building destroyed by Hurricane Camille. The USO had the building moved forward slightly, and then the National USO of New York renovated and furnished it.

The City of Biloxi obtained rights for the Dantzler House, all equipment and furnishings in 1976. This occurred after the USO agency was discontinued. The Biloxi Parks and Recreation Department then used it as administration offices. In later years, it was rented as office space as well as used by other City of Biloxi departments.

In 1998, the City of Biloxi's tricentennial committee used the Dantzler house as its home base. The home was used for tricentennial administration offices, for committee meetings and as a planning area. After a very successful tricentennial celebration, the building was once more used for City of Biloxi office space.

The house's most recent history had to do with the Mardi Gras Museum, which was located in the Magnolia Hotel. The decision was made to move it from the Magnolia Hotel to the Dantzler House. This appeared to be a great move for the museum, the Dantzler House and the lighthouse. The threefold attractions would appeal to tourists and locals alike. All of these historic draws appeared to be headed into a successful year. Unfortunately, Hurricane Katrina made its appearance and not only destroyed the Dantzler House but also some precious Mardi Gras costumes, pictures and memorabilia. Today, the Biloxi Lighthouse Visitor Center, built to look similar to the Dantzler House, sits on this property.

5

Father Ryan House

For many years, tourists driving along Highway 90 in Biloxi were amazed to see a home that had a palm tree growing in the center of the front porch staircase. Some let their curiosity overwhelm them, so they would stop and ask one of the locals about it and take a few pictures to show their families back home. Like so many landmarks along the Gulf Coast, the Father Ryan House became a favorite tourist stop. In the later years, the home became a bed-and-breakfast. Unfortunately, like so many other landmarks, Hurricane Katrina turned it into a pile of debris.

Historically, the home was known as the Wade House and was located at 1196 Beach Boulevard, old 428 West Beach Boulevard. Judge W.C. Wade bought the property in 1838, and sometime between 1840 and 1841, the home was built. The property value in 1840 was $112, but in 1841, the value was up to $1,000, indicating that there was some type of structure on the property. The Wade family sold the home to Harriet Louise Hobbs for $2,500. The fact that it had a higher dollar value in 1843 is a strong indication that at the time of its assessment in 1841, the home was not completed. Harriet Hobbs's husband was listed as John Watt, who was originally from Natchez but was later listed in New Orleans. John Watt was a merchant in the cotton industry and was listed in New Orleans from 1849 to 1866.

In 1855, a hurricane hit the Mississippi Gulf Coast. Many wharfs and bathhouses were swept away, including John Watts and Harriet Hobbs's wharf and bathhouse. The *Daily Picayune* reported very few homes

The Father Ryan House with a young palm tree protruding from the steps. *Courtesy of the Alan Santa Cruz Collection.*

destroyed along the Mississippi Gulf Coast. John and Harriet, like so many fellow New Orleanians, were most likely using their Mississippi Gulf Coast home as a summer home.

In 1885, after the death of John, Harriet sold the property to Thomas W. Carter, who was a New Orleans architect. Carter was born in London, England, and had arrived in the United States about 1870. Carter eventually moved to New Orleans, where he became a prominent architect in the Crescent City for about fifteen years. In 1885, he purchased the Wade House and retired to the Mississippi Gulf Coast. It is believed that Carter made alterations to the home that made it stand out from other beachfront homes. The addition of rooms on the second floor altered the roofline. The home also had dormers across the front and rear of the roof. The rear dormers were part of the original home, while the ones in front were added at a later date.

The Wade House was most recently known as the Father Ryan House, and Biloxi also has a street named Father Ryan Avenue, but who was Father

Ryan? He is sometimes called the Poet Priest of the Confederacy and Poet Laureate of the South. Either way, he became a great American poet.

Father Abram J. Ryan's parents were Matthew Ryan and Mary Coughlin, both immigrants from Ireland. There has been some dispute about his birth and birthplace. Proof of Father Ryan's birth in Hagerstown comes from a letter written by Bishop O'Connell, the bishop of Richmond, Virginia. The letter was addressed to the clergy of St. Mary's Parish in Hagerstown and dated 1910. The bishop indicated that this was the second time he had written to inform the parish that the poet/priest was born in his parish. He also wrote that this information came from the lips of Father Ryan himself during a conversation with Father Hugh McKeefry at Norfolk. These records indicated that Abram J. Ryan was born on February 5, 1838, in Hagerstown, Maryland.

Sometime after Father Ryan's birth, the Ryan family migrated to St. Louis, Missouri, where Father Ryan attended the Christian Brothers School. One source indicates he began his studies for the priesthood in 1854 at New York State, but the records of the St. Vincent de Paul rectory indicate he started in Germantown, Philadelphia. He was ordained a Vincentian priest on November 1, 1856. He left the Vincentian community on September 1, 1862, and returned to Missouri to teach. After the outbreak of the Civil War, he volunteered to attend to spiritual needs of the Confederate army.

During many battles, he ministered to dying and injured Confederate and Federal soldiers. One London writer attached to General Braggs's army at Missionary Ridge and Lookout Mountain reported that Father Ryan was loved by all Southern soldiers, whether they were Catholic, Protestant or Jewish. Even though they knew he detested slavery, they knew he loved the South. General Grant was in charge of the Federal forces opposing General Bragg. Soon Grant was tearing Bragg's army to pieces. During the 1864 battle at Franklin, Tennessee, Father Ryan ministered to the dead and dying for at least ten hours. When an unnamed newspaper reporter found Father Ryan, he was ministering among the dead and dying, and he indicated that he was praying these words to God:

> *Oh gracious God will not this sacrifice satisfy Thy wrath. Look with pity on Thy erring people.*

All that Father Ryan witnessed during the Civil War and in its aftermath, he soon put to pen and paper. This earned him the title of Poet Laureate of the South. While serving as chaplain for the Confederate army, Father

The Father Ryan House was a tourist attraction during the 1960s. *Courtesy of the Alan Santa Cruz Collection.*

Ryan received news that Robert E. Lee had surrendered. Knowing that the war was at its end, he penned the poem "The Conquered Banner." After the end of the hostilities, Father Ryan began serving in parishes in Louisiana, Tennessee, Georgia, Alabama and Mississippi. While in New Orleans, he served as editor of the *Star*, a Catholic weekly. In Augusta, Georgia, he founded the *Banner of the South*, a religious and political weekly.

About 1870, after a very active career, he moved to Mobile, Alabama, where he served the Diocese of Mobile. By this time, several volumes of his verses had been published. During this time, the yellow fever epidemic gripped the South. Father Ryan experienced the epidemic firsthand. Moved by all the sorrow around him, he placed it in verse:

> *Around me blight, where all before was bloom, and so much loss—and nothing won. Save this—that I can kneel on dust and tomb. And weep-and weeping, pray, Thy will be done.*

During the 1880s, he lectured in several northern cities. Some of his lectures were about aspects of modern civilization and religious themes. While in Baltimore, his book *Poems: Patriotic, Religious, and Miscellaneous* was published.

Accounts published in 1886 in a Washington, D.C. paper indicate that Jefferson Davis gave a public speech at Mississippi City about 1879. After Jefferson Davis's speech, Father Ryan came forward. Addressing Jefferson Davis and all within hearing distance, he indicated that he thanked God that Jefferson Davis's thinking had not been altered like the mandatory reconstruction had altered the South. This was Father Ryan's, the poet, way of recognizing that Jefferson Davis, the great statesman, had not been changed by war or reconstruction.

By 1881, he had returned to Mobile. Having serviced the Mobile diocese with hard and faithful work for eleven years, Father Ryan's health became an issue. Bishop John Quinlan reported in a letter dated October 19, 1881, that Father Ryan's physician has advised him to live somewhere on the coast to help prolong his life. He indicated that Father Ryan wished to be in Biloxi, Mississippi, or somewhere nearby. The article indicates that he had leased a pretty place in Biloxi known as the Wade House. The bishop indicated that he was not releasing Ryan from the diocese, and Ryan would have to report to him once a month. On March 10, 1882, Ryan wrote a letter to Jefferson Davis addressed from Biloxi. There is some debate about how long Father Ryan stayed in Biloxi, but without newspaper accounts or other documentation, this may never be resolved.

Father Ryan continued to be active until April 22, 1886, when he passed away at a Franciscan monastery in Louisville, Kentucky. His body was returned to Mobile, where he was laid to rest in St. Mary's Cemetery. In 1912, a drive was launched in Mobile to erect a memorial in his honor. In July 1913, it was dedicated with a stanza from his poem "The Conquered Banner." It was also engraved "Poet, Patriot, and Priest." Father Ryan wrote two poems while in Biloxi. They were "Sea Rest" and "Sea Reverie."

The home was typical of most of the beachfront homes of that period with the exception of the roof. The roof was a combination of different styles of architecture. The design created living space in the roof area, now the second floor. Dormers across the front and back of the home provided good circulation and an abundance of light. The three dormers across the front each had a balcony and French doors. The center dormer was twice as wide as the other two and also had a glass observatory built on top.

In 1978, the *Daily Herald* reported that the Father Ryan House was being restored. The restoration of the first floor was almost complete, and in time, the second floor would be restored. Mr. and Mrs. John O'Keefe had purchased the home in 1976 and were restoring it to its original nineteenth-century appearance. The wooden floors on the first floor had to be replaced

Father Abram J. Ryan. *Courtesy of the Lynn and Sandra Patterson Collection.*

and the walls restored. After the restoration, the O'Keefe family furnished the home with nineteenth-century furniture. The first floor had six rooms with two fireplaces and the second floor three rooms and attic space. The O'Keefe family eventually sold the home. Rosanne and Jefferson McKenney turned it into a bed-and-breakfast.

Of course, like other historical sites, the Father Ryan House was not without its legend. The legend indicates that Father Ryan had placed a wrought-iron cross in the middle of the outside staircase. After Father Ryan's death in 1886, the cross disappeared; yet, in the same spot, a palm tree began to grow. The home was noted for this palm.

The Father Ryan House was considered one of the most important structures in Biloxi. Then, on August 29, Hurricane Katrina reduced the house to rubble, with only the famous palm tree still standing. The final insult came when the palm tree was cut down in 2014.

6

Fisherman's Cottage

Before Katrina, a new restaurant, called Hobnob Café, had opened in the old Fisherman's Cottage that was located at 122 Lameuse. Things appeared to be going well for the new café. Then, Katrina in all its fury reduced the structure to piles of wood. The Fisherman's Cottage had originally been located at 262 (today 643) Bayview Avenue. The exact date of its construction is not know, but it was listed in the 1905 city directory with the Martin Fountain family was residing at this location. Though not proven, local tradition says that Martin Fountain built the home before the 1905 date.

In the 1913 and '14 city directories, the Fountain family was still residing at this location. In 1925, Walter Fountain Sr. and his wife, Winnie, were listed as residents of the home. Walter was the brother of Martin Fountain. The directory listed Walter Fountain Sr. as a factory foreman at Foster Fountain Company, boat builders. His duties included taking care of the Foster Fountain Company's fleet of boats. After the Fountain family, local canning companies owned the Fisherman's Cottage. The building finally came under the ownership of the Gollott family, which owned a seafood factory with an oil dock and nearby transfer and storage companies.

On April 4, 1981, the *Daily Herald* reported that Representative Tommy Gollott had made a presentation to Biloxi mayor Jerry O'Keefe and the city council. Representative Gollott, on behalf of the Gollott family, offered the Fisherman's Cottage as a gift to the city. The *Daily Herald* reported

The Fisherman's Cottage facing Lameuse Street. *Courtesy of the City of Biloxi.*

The Fisherman's Cottage, side profile. *Courtesy of the City of Biloxi.*

that the cottage was a Creole-type house, the only one in Biloxi with two entrance doors in the exterior bays.

Mayor O'Keefe accepted the gift from the Gollott family and described the cottage as having a lot of character. He also said he hoped the city would be able to accept the special gift and preserve it and other local buildings from the early days of Biloxi. The city council said that it would have to seek bids for the removal and indicated that the grounds of the Tullis-Toledano Manor was possibly a good location for this structure. But it was not moved to Tullis-Toledano Manor; it was moved to 122 Lameuse Street and was being used as a commercial building.

The Fisherman's Cottage had some of the most exceptionally decorated exterior woodwork in Biloxi. The front gallery—with its sunburst relief patterns and rows of discs and pendants in the center—was very ornate. All this woodwork carefully came together to create the beautiful arches along the gallery columns. This was a one-of-a-kind structure influenced directly by Biloxi's history. The center of the building appears to have been an original building with additions added around the original building. Like so many other historical structures, the Fisherman's Cottage could not stand up to the wind and waters of Hurricne Katrina. The structure is gone, but its history will endure.

7

Pleasant Reed House

Before Hurricane Katrina, many individuals were anticipating the opening of the new Ohr-O'Keefe Museum of Art. It was beginning to take shape under beautiful oak trees. The Ohr-O'Keefe buildings formed a campus that would house the artwork of artists from all walks of life. The buildings themselves were meant to be works of art. In the midst of these buildings sat the Pleasant Reed House. Built by a former slave, the Pleasant Reed House was to become the centerpiece of an African American art exhibit on the campus.

However, Hurricane Katrina pounded the site of the Ohr-O'Keefe Museum of Art, causing severe damage to the new buildings and reducing the Pleasant Reed house to splinters and bricks. Like so many historic homes from the National Register of Historic Places, the Pleasant Reed House was no match for the storm.

The house was built by Pleasant Reed, a former slave. Pleasant Reed was born in 1854 to Benjamin and Charlotte Reed. He was the fourth of eleven children. The Reed family members were slaves of John B. Reed. The Reed farm was located on the Leaf River in Perry County, Mississippi. Pleasant was born before the Civil War, which, about ten years later, made him and the rest of the Reed family free.

It didn't take the Reed family members long to begin utilizing their new freedom. Many former slaves wanted to leave plantation life in the past. They began seeking other avenues to earn a living and make better lives for their families. In 1896, nineteen-year-old George Reed Sr., Pleasant's older

The Pleasant Reed House on the Ohr-O'Keefe Museum campus before Hurricane Katrina. *Author's collection.*

brother, migrated to the Mississippi Gulf Coast. In short order, the rest of the Reed family began to do the same. George settled in Biloxi, which, at that time, had a population of about three thousand. By 1871, the entire family was living in Biloxi. That same year, Harrison County listed three members of the family as paying taxes. Benjamin Reed, Pleasant's father, is listed as the owner of four head of cattle.

The Mississippi Gulf Coast has been influenced by French and Spanish laws and culture and by the New Orleanians who visit Mississippi's Gulf Coast. The coast's culture is unlike any other part of Mississippi, and the area had become a tourist trap long before the term was coined. Of course, salt breezes and saltwater were long thought to have healthful qualities that could heal stress and improve one's overall health. The Civil War shut down tourism, but it did not take long for the industry to begin building back up. Another good quality of the Gulf Coast is the accessibility of a wide variety of seafood that can be gathered by anyone willing to work for it.

The Reed family may have felt that the combination of tourism business and the availability of seafood would afford them the new opportunities they were seeking. Pleasant arrived in Biloxi and began working as a carpenter in the business and residential sectors. He soon became a jack-of-all-trades. Pleasant also learned net-making skills from his brother Benjamin, who was a local fisherman. Pleasant Reed married Georgia Anna Harris in 1884, and from this union, five children would be born.

In 1886, Pleasant Reed purchased a 50- by 104-foot lot from Jacob Elmer. Pleasant made a working agreement with Elmer and, in four years, had paid for the property. His father, Benjamin Reed, also purchased a lot nearby. The street would later be known as Elmer Street. Pleasant must have begun construction of his home shortly after its purchase because by 1887, the structure was completed. He had used the shotgun style for his home but added a side hallway. The side hall is found in large numbers in New Orleans.

There is some oral family history that indicates the older family members spoke a French dialect. The family tree may have originated on a Louisiana plantation, and from that plantation, French-speaking family members were sold to John Reed, a Mississippi plantation owner. This would account for the use of the French dialect and the architectural style used in the construction of the Pleasant Reed House. During this period, kitchens were built as

A side view of a replica of the Pleasant Reed House on the Ohr-O'Keefe Museum campus, 2015. *Author's collection.*

separate structures for two reasons: one, of course, was the heat produced while cooking; the other was the fact that kitchens easily caught fire.

In 1886, the City of Biloxi rented a house from the Colored Baptist Church on Main Street and turned it into the first Colored Public School in Biloxi. The Reed family placed a high value on education, and the Reed children most likely attended this school.

Around 1894, a one-and-a-half-story clapboard section was added to the rear of the Pleasant Reed House. Later, an additional room and gallery were added but were eventually removed. During World War I, two of Pleasant and Georgia's sons, Paul and Percy, like so many young men of that time, joined the military. Both married locally and settled in Biloxi. In one city directory, Percy was listed as a laborer and Paul as a boatman. One Reed daughter, Theresa, would continue to live with her parents and care for them as they aged. Family oral history indicates that, at one time, Theresa was engaged to a fisherman who died before their marriage. Tragedy struck the Reed family again on June 2, 1933, when Georgia passed away. On February 4, 1936, Pleasant passed away. In his obituary, the *Biloxi Daily Herald* indicated that he was well known in Biloxi by white and black Biloxians.

The Reed family continued to own the Pleasant Reed House until September 12, 1978, when a new chapter began for the home. By this time, the home had deteriorated and would have been demolished if the Gulf Coast chapter of Delta Sigma Theta Sorority had not realized the historical value of the home. The Pleasant Reed House was sold to the Mississippi alumni chapter of Delta Sigma Theta Sorority, Inc. for ten dollars. It was then placed on the National Register of Historic Places. The sorority realized that the home would continue to deteriorate and would be lost if something wasn't done soon. The sorority members worked very hard to have the home restored, but the battle was tough. Then, through an alliance with the Ohr-O'Keefe Museum of Art, another new chapter began to unfold for the Pleasant Reed House.

The board of trustees of the Ohr-O'Keefe Museum of Art voted to make the Pleasant Reed House the centerpiece of the African American Art Wing. The Pleasant Reed House was relocated from Elmer Street to the site of the Ohr-O'Keefe Museum of Art. The restoration work brought the home back to its early 1887 appearance. Like the Fisherman's Cottage, the Pleasant Reed House would showcase the living conditions of common Biloxi families.

Another wonderful aspect of the Pleasant Reed House was its contents. The Reed family had preserved records of family transactions dating back to

A front view of the replica of the Pleasant Reed House on the Ohr-O'Keefe Museum campus, 2015. *Author's collection.*

1884. The documents included grocery receipts, rent receipts, doctor's bills and agreements of items purchased. Some of the most unusual receipts are for time performing roadwork in exchange for tax payments. These documents served as great educational tools to understanding the life of the common man in 1800s Biloxi. The documents and home shed light on the Reed family's rise from slavery to create their own cultural legacy.

Everything was looking up for the Pleasant Reed House and the Ohr-O'Keefe Museum of Art until Hurricane Katrina intervened. The Ohr-O'Keefe Museum suffered a large setback, and the Pleasant Reed House was completely destroyed. Like so many other organizations that suffered thanks to Katrina, the Ohr-O'Keefe board of trustees is determined to complete the museum.

One bright spot I learned about while talking to Marjie Gowdy is that the board of trustees of the Ohr-O'Keefe Museum of Art voted in the spring of 2006 to build a replica of the Pleasant Reed House. There had been a debate among historians about whether it was worth replicating a building that was historically significant because of the person who built it. After much consultation around the community and the nation, the board decided that the most important thing was to honor the legacy of Pleasant

Reed as an independent workingman freed from slavery and that his legacy was best preserved in a replica of his house.

While furnishings within the house were lost in the hurricane, Curator Dora Faison saved most of the archival materials and original photographs before the storm. Hurricane Katrina tried to wipe away our history, but the determination of Biloxians helped preserve the legacy of the Pleasant Reed House. Today, a replica of the Pleasant Reed House sits on the Ohr-O'Keefe Museum campus.

8

Old Mud Daub House

Biloxi's Oldest Home

I guess this is one of those stories that should begin with "once upon a time." As we know, most "once upon a time" stories are fantasy, but this one, unfortunately, is true. It's the sad story of history lost due to a clash between progress and preservation of a landmark. It sounds like recent history, when so much development and progress threatens historical and archaeological landmarks. However, this drama took place in the 1930s in the city of Biloxi.

The structure was an old mud daub house that was believed to have been built in the 1700s. A group of historic-minded Biloxi citizens was interested in preserving its history. Feeling that the house was in danger of being torn down, the citizens started a drive to save it. Through hard work, they convinced the city to purchase the site and the old mud daub house. The land and house cost the city $1,000. If the story ended here, it would be a fantasy story, but soon developers were eying the property, and a battle between progress and preservation began. Unfortunately, developers convinced the city leaders that progress was better than saving a precious landmark of the past. With the stroke of a pen, the oldest house in the Mississippi Valley was condemned.

Why was this house so important? When was it built? Who built it? Let's take a look at the history of the old mud daub house and the Porter Avenue area. To do this, we have to roll back time and travel to the 1700s, the French period.

On October 26, 1719, the superior council, the colony's governing body, decided to relocate its capital back to Old Biloxi (Ocean Springs). Across

The old Mud Daub House was Biloxi's oldest home. Its historic marker is pictured in the inset. *Courtesy of the Alan Santa Cruz Collection.*

the bay from Old Biloxi was New Biloxi (Biloxi). Here, some years before, a Canadian man named Deslots had established a settlement. In a short period of time, French concessions, or land grants, would line Biloxi's shoreline.

By late 1720, the capital had been moved from Old Biloxi to New Biloxi to a ravine that was located on the west side of Porter Avenue. Plans were drawn to build Fort Louis on that site. The fort's earthen works were started. But the fort was never completed. By 1722, Governor Jean Baptiste Lemoyne de Bienville began his efforts to move the capital to New Orleans. On February 1, 1723, the capital of Louisiana was officially moved from Biloxi to New Orleans. A garrison of six men commanded by a sergeant was detailed for the post at Biloxi.

The memoirs of Charles Le Gac, director of the Compagnie des Indes in Louisiana, indicate that in early 1721, about 2,129 individuals had debarked at New Biloxi. Eventually, nine concessions, numbering about 250 individuals each, lined Biloxi's shoreline. They cleared the land and built cabins and warehouses.

During the French colonial period, the settlers at New Biloxi had built warehouses and cabins. In fact, each concession had built its own warehouses and cabins, as well as the company warehouses. Was the old mud daub house one of these cabins? Were these structures torn down when the operation was moved to New Orleans? There is no way to be sure, but most likely the structures remained because a military post was left at this location and there were still a few settlers left.

The center of the French establishment of Biloxi had been Porter Avenue. The concessions that had lined Biloxi beaches were those of M. Le Blanc (minister of war), John Law, Sieur de Meuse, Sieur de Chaumont, Sieur de Paris du Vernay, Sieur de Coly, Sieur Du Manoir, Sieur Villemont, M. Clerac and Sieur D'artaguette.

The Le Blanc concession, today the location of the Biloxi Lighthouse Visitors Center, was most likely located at the northeast corner of Porter Avenue and Beach Boulevard. It is very possible that the old mud daub, or bousillage, house was one of Le Blanc concession's structures. We do know that French burials have been found in this location beginning in 1914. To date, thirty-three French burials have been excavated, researched and reinterred on the visitors' center's grounds.

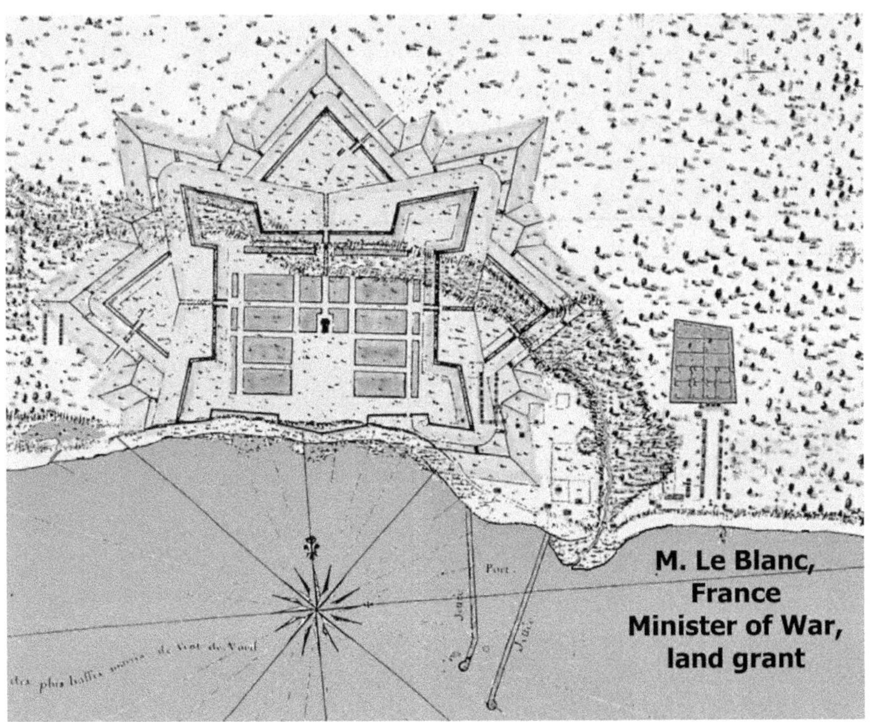

M. Le Blanc's, French Minister of War, land grant on Biloxi's beach, 1720. *Courtesy of the Maritime and Seafood Industry Museum.*

Bousillage construction was used in France and French-colonial Louisiana. The bousillage was a mixture of mud or clay, cured Spanish moss or straw and animal hair or fur, if available. After the house was framed, wooden sticks, braced six to eight inches apart, were placed between diagonal and horizontal wood timber. The bousillage, clay and Spanish moss, was draped over the sticks and then packed until even with wooden beams. According to descriptions and pictures, the old mud daub house appears to have been constructed in the same manner.

Unfortunately, city leaders and developers saw only the old building and not the jewel that could have drawn tourists and historical scholars. As far as our lost history, it is only lost if we allow it to be lost. There are still pictures, historical documents, films and written history. Our history gives us a sense of place, a sense of belonging and a sense of pride. The old mud daub house on Porter Avenue has physically faded into history but not from memory. As long as someone tells the story and someone listens, the old mud daub house will live forever.

9

Old Brick House

For years, one of Biloxi's oldest structures, the old brick house, was nestled between lumber mills, shipyards and seafood factories. Like so many other structures, Katrina took its toll on the old brick house. This was not the first time it laid in disrepair.

Known architecturally as the Rodgers House, the old brick house is located at 622 Bayview Avenue. The structure dates to the mid-nineteenth century. The first known records of the property can be found in the Spanish land grants. In 1784, Jean Baptiste Carquotte was granted 285.73 acres by the Spanish provincial government; this included the property of the Old Brick House. In 1824, Carquotte died. In 1843, his heirs sold the property to William Rodgers from New Orleans. In 1850, Rodgers died, and per the instructions in his will, the property was sold and the proceeds were donated to the Poor Boys' Asylum in New Orleans.

The purchaser was John L. Henley, and he lived at this location until 1872. During the 1860s, there were three other brick structures in Biloxi—the Friedlander home, the Toledano Manor and the Elmer home on Magnolia. During the Civil War, Henley was placed in charge of Biloxi defenses. There was little manpower left in Biloxi with most of the men away fighting the war. Still, Henley and his supporters did keep the Union troops at bay by using Quaker (fake) cannons placed in a battery near the lighthouse. On New Year's Eve 1862, Union troops came ashore at Biloxi under a flag of truce. After realizing the gun battery was nothing more than logs painted black and one useless cannon, they demanded the mayor surrender Biloxi.

The Old Brick House, Bay View Avenue, 1950s. *Courtesy of the Alan Santa Cruz Collection.*

Union command soon realized there was little or no threat at Biloxi and left the city alone. Henley was considered a war hero by local people and was elected mayor of Biloxi after the war.

In 1872, Henley sold the old brick house to Jacob Elmer. Elmer only owned the property for six years. In 1878, he sold it to Dr. Edward Bell of New Orleans. The Bell family, like so many other New Orleans families, used the old brick house as a summer home. Dr. Bell's family would own the property until 1921. For the next thirty years, it functioned as a machine shop, a warehouse and a seafood factory office. It then lay abandoned, with the exception of a short occupation by the Works Progress Administration's adult education program. It laid abandoned for so long that rumors and legends about it being haunted began to surface. In 1951, the numerous garden clubs from Woolmarket, Biloxi, North Biloxi (St. Martin and D'Iberville communities) and Ocean Springs convinced the city to lease them the property, and the home became the Biloxi Garden Center. The old brick house was no longer abandoned or haunted; it had a new beginning.

In 1952, the Biloxi Garden Center was incorporated and began the restoration project. This project became a long labor of love. Most of the restoration was completed by 1966, and that same year, the property

Hurricane Katrina left gaping holes in the Old Brick House, 2005. *Author's collection.*

was deeded to the Biloxi Garden Center by the City of Biloxi. Due to the club's efforts, the home was once again a center for social activities and special events. The architecture of the old brick house is a blend of American and French colonial traditions. Anyone familiar with the Toledano House will note the similarities between the two structures. The old brick house was only one and a half stories with a staircase rising from the rear gallery.

Though some of the interior trim may not have been original to the house, it was still graceful and historic. The six-panel doors downstairs were most likely original, as were the boarded ceilings. During Hurricanes Camille and Katrina, the main gallery was destroyed. After Camille and Katrina, it was historically restored. When viewing the house from Bay View Avenue, it is important to remember that the front of it faces the bay.

The original rear gallery was enclosed during the 1920s. The main entrance had double doors with a sidelight, or glass panels. The glass panels were located in the pilasters—ornamental columns protruding from the walls—on both sides of the double doors. Halfway between the main entrance and the ends of the house were two additional solid wood doors. At one time, the home had a detached kitchen with a covered overhang between the house and kitchen.

The remodeled Old Brick House, rear view, 2012. *Author's collection.*

The remodeled Old Brick House, front gallery facing the Back Bay of Biloxi, 2012. *Author's collection.*

In the 1920s, Bay View Avenue was being developed, and the kitchen was dismantled. The old brick house was one of about seventy-two Mississippi properties that were on the National Register of historic places before Katrina.

The Old Brick House felt the full fury of Hurricane Katrina, which left a gaping hole in the center of the house. It suffered a terrible blow but was restored. Today, folks are once again able to sit on its front gallery and view the beautiful Biloxi Bay.

10

Old Spanish House

Nestled in the old section of downtown Biloxi is a structure whose history is full of fact and legend. This structure was known architecturally as the Scherer House but known locally as the Old Spanish House. The Old Spanish House is located at 782 Water Street. It sits just north of Mary Mahoney's Restaurant, between G.E. Ohr Street and the Rue Magnolia.

Sometimes, legends begin as rumors, and historical facts are added to make them more believable. As far as the Old Spanish House goes, part of the legend indicates that it was located in the colonial area of the city. During the French colonial period, some of the concessions were located in this section of the city. The legend says that the Old Spanish House was built shortly after 1780 by a Spanish army captain. Said captain was to be commandant of the Biloxi area. The building was supposedly built as a military headquarters, barracks and social and religious center for the outpost. Historical facts indicate that districts were setup in the Bay of St. Louis and Pascagoula during the Spanish period. In 1805, Juan Bautista Pellerin was commander in the Bay of St. Louis, and the capital of Spanish West Florida was located at Pensacola. During the Spanish period, neither military post nor any military personnel were located in the Biloxi area, which was under the Bay St. Louis district.

Now, let's look at the real history of the Old Spanish House and its property. The structure was most likely built in the mid-1840s. John

The Old Spanish House. *Courtesy of the Alan Santa Cruz Collection.*

The Old Spanish House, rear view, 2015. *Author's collection.*

The Old Spanish House, front view, 2015. *Author's collection.*

Delauney owned the property before 1839. Delauney sold the property to Eliza Ladnier in 1839. Ladnier sold the property to Arne and Adelle Bernard in 1843 for $1,000. In 1846, the Bernards sold a portion of the property to Pierre Danjean for $600. Three months later, Danjean divided the property and sold the section with the house for $1,000. It was believed that Danjean had begun the construction of the house, which was not completed when the property was sold. The new owners were C.H. Kaufamn and H. Fritz, cabinetmakers from Germany. Kaufamn and Fritz finished the Old Spanish House and are credited with building it. When the Magnolia Hotel was built, Kaufamn was the contractor. Fritz supposedly built the first water-powered sawmill in Pineville. Pineville is located just north of Delisle. He is also credited with building many homes in the Woolmarket area.

The Old Spanish House faces Water Street, which was also constructed in the 1840s. In Mobile and New Orleans, similar houses were built in the 1830s and 1840s. The stepped gables and narrow balconies are very unusual features and are possibly what fueled the legend that it was built by Spaniards in 1780s. The house is also unusual since it is two stories and brick. The only other two-storied houses were the Tullis-Toledano

House, which was also brick, and the wooden Bailey House (old Holy Angels Nursery). Katrina destroyed the latter two, but the Old Spanish House escaped Hurricane Katrina's full rage. With so many lost and damaged structures, the Old Spanish House will be a gem for many generations.

11

Gunston Hall/White Pillars

Many of us remember the White Pillars Restaurant. Of course, we are all currently watching the remodeling of this historic restaurant and cannot wait to enter its door and eat there again. What we do not know is the history of this house or the history of three families who lived there. Gunston Hall was one of the last of the grand houses built on Biloxi's beachfront. It was built in the Classical Revival style of the period. The home was built by Dr. Hyman Folkes and his wife, Theresa Lopez, in 1920.

Hyman McMackin Folkes was born on October 6, 1871, in Bovina, Mississippi. Today, Bovina is an unincorporated community near Vicksburg in Warren County. Dr. Folkes received his medical degree from Tulane University in 1894. In 1895, he went to Guatemala as a surgeon for the Varapaz Railroad Company. The Varapaz Railroad was organized and built by German immigrants in Guatemala. Its purpose was to transport coffee from the German farms to Port of Panzos, which had access to the Caribbean Sea.

Due to poor health, Dr. Folkes returned to the United States in 1897. On his return, he accepted a position in the quarantine office at the Ship Island Quarantine Station. During the yellow fever outbreak in late 1897, he evacuated to Biloxi but still contracted the disease. In Biloxi, he was elected coast sanitary inspector by the state board of health and served for one term. Here, he opened his own private practice in 1898. Eventually, he became a partner in the drug firm of Folkes & Grant Company.

In Biloxi, Dr. Folkes met Theresa Lopez, the daughter of Lazaro and Julia Lopez. Lazaro was one of the original developers of Biloxi's seafood industry. He helped organize Lopez, Elmer and Company, the first seafood canning company on the Mississippi Gulf Coast. In 1884, after withdrawing from the company, Lazaro and W.K.M. Dukate joined forces with the Dunbar family and created Lopez, Dunbar's Sons and Company. Lazaro was a generous and prominent citizen of Biloxi.

On June 4, 1900, Dr. Hyman Folkes and Theresa Lopez were married. On June 10, the *Times-Picayune* ran a story on what it deemed the main social event of the week, the marriage of Theresa Lopez to Dr. Hyman McMackin Folkes at the church of the Nativity of the Blessed Virgin Mary in Biloxi, Mississippi. The bridesmaids were Erena Lopez, May Young and Jennie Gillen. The best man was William Wackenfeld. It was reported that the young couple left Biloxi with good wishes. Their honeymoon was an extended tour through New York State and other

Gunston Hall, early 1900s. *Courtesy of the Alan Santa Cruz Collection.*

eastern states. On their return, they made their home in Biloxi. Also in 1900, Mississippi governor Andrew Houston Longino appointed Dr. Hyman Folkes to represent Mississippi on the Yellow Fever Commission.

Dr. Folkes traveled to Cuba as a commission member. In Cuba, Carlos Finlay, a Cuban doctor, had a theory that yellow fever was transmitted by mosquitoes. Major Walter Reed and the commission confirmed this theory, which helped in the fight against yellow fever. This also helped with the completion of the work on the Panama Canal. Major Reed gave Dr. Carlos Finlay credit for the discovery, but Major Reed became the hero of the yellow fever fight and was given a lot of the credit. Today, Walter Reed Army Medical Center is named after Major Reed.

During this period, it was believed that natural mineral springs, salt breezes and saltwater helped clean the mind and body from the filthy environment of the big cities. Dr. Folkes was one of the advocates of this school of thought, and he believed Biloxi was one of the healthiest places. With this in mind, he built the Biloxi Sanatorium.

The 1900s facility was up-to-date with rooms as comfortable as a hotel. The facility had an operating room, a complete X-ray lab and a glassed-in roof garden. The facility had a heated pool and offered Turkish, Russian, mineral and natural saltwater baths. His staff of nurses and trained attendants made sure that the patients received ample sunlight, sea breezes and saltwater.

In 1904, a fire destroyed the sanatorium and nine homes. Dr. Folkes rebuilt his facility. In 1908, Mississippi governor Edmond Noel named Dr. Folkes one of the representatives to the International Congress on Tuberculosis. In 1909, Dr. Folkes announced that his Biloxi Sanatorium would become a modern tourist hotel. This would be the Biloxi Hotel, today the Chateau le Grand.

On the corner of Beach Boulevard and Rodenberg Avenue, Hyman and Theresa Folkes built their home in 1920. The structure was styled after an old Virginia plantation home and was named Gunston Hall. Folkes may have done this to memorialize George Mason's Virginia home of the same name.

On May 1, 1928, Dr. Hyman Folkes had a stroke and died at Gunston Hall. The *Times-Picayune* reported that he was survived by his wife and two daughters, Josephine and Anna Folkes. The May 2 article praised Dr. Folkes for being influential in the organization and maintenance of the Biloxi city hospital. He was also considered one of Biloxi's most significant citizens.

Between 1936 and 1940, Theresa Lopez Folkes moved from Gunston Hall to 1306 Beach Boulevard, which was next door to the Biloxi Hotel. On July 26, 1951, Theresa Folkes passed away and was laid to rest next to her beloved husband.

The story of Harry and Julia Wendt will remind you of a dramatic novel or an old black-and-white film. It has romance, adventure, tragedy, misfortune and, finally, triumph. Harry and Julia purchased Gunston Hall in 1940 during a visit to Biloxi. They most likely purchased Gunston Hall directly from Theresa Lopez Folkes.

Harry Wendt was born on March 5, 1892, in German, Ohio, to Arthur Wendt and Catherine Fettee. Harry attended Wittenberg College in Springfield, Ohio. While earning a teaching degree, he was active in the Beta Theta Pi fraternity and played varsity football and ran track. After graduating from college in 1916, he boarded a ship for Manila, Philippines, to do educational work. Some of his plans included traveling to Japan for the Olympic meet and vacationing in China.

Julia Kipping was born on October 4, 1896, in Carrolton County, Kentucky. While little is known about Julia's early life, she did go to school and list her occupation as teacher on her U.S. passport. In 1920, she boarded the ship *Empress of Asia* for Manila, Philippines. She also had plans to visit Japan, Hong Kong and China. She returned to the United States, and in 1922, she once again journeyed to Manila. Harry and Julia were on a course of fate that would change their lives. On August 11, 1924, Harry traveled to Hong Kong to do a little business and also to vacation. At the same time, Julia Kipping was also visiting Hong Kong and indicated on her U.S. passport that her residence was in Wilson, North Carolina.

On August 19, the American consular service in Hong Kong documented the marriage of Harry Alden Wendt to Julia Kipping. They were married at the Cathedral of St. John in Victoria, Hong Kong. It is unknown exactly how or where the two met, but it most likely happened in the Philippines, Japan or China. One way or another, they had been mostly corresponding by mail. The married couple returned to the Philippines to make their home. Over the course of time, both would become teachers at the Santo Tomas University in Manila.

Both visited the United States from time to time. During one visit, on May 24, 1940, Julia arrived at the harbor of San Pedro, California. Her passport indicated that she was journeying to Coleman Vista in Gulfport, Mississippi. While staying in Gulfport, she purchased Gunston Hall on West Beach in Biloxi, Mississippi.

A side view of the restored Gunston Hall, also known as White Pillars, 2015. *Author's collection.*

In 1940, Julia began the task of preparing the new home for Harry and herself. On March 27, 1941, Harry Wendt died in Manila, Philippines, never to live in the new home. It was most likely days before Julia received the heartbreaking news and began planning her journey back to the Philippines to handle her husband's affairs. Little did she know, she would not return to her beloved Gunston Hall for four years.

On April 3, she boarded the plane the Honolulu Clipper for the last leg of her journey to Manila. Once in the Philippines, she began the task of selling the Wendt property and belongings and settling Harry's affairs.

The Japanese attack on Pearl Harbor on December 7 occurred while Julia was still in Manila on Luzon Island. On December 8, the Japanese invasion of the Luzon Island began. By January 2, Manila had fallen to the Japanese. Julia was captured that same day and, along with 4,700 others, was placed in a prisoner-of-war camp at Santo Tomas University. Julia found herself imprisoned at the same university where she had taught English. Among the civilian prisoners were 3,200 Americans and 900 British, including Austrians and Canadians. The group also included citizens of Poland, Holland, Spain, Mexico, Nicaragua, Cuba, Russia, Belgium, Sweden, Denmark, China and Burma. By May 6, the Philippines had surrendered to Japanese forces. In the beginning, the conditions, though not ideal, were better than some Japanese prisoner-of-war camps. By 1944, that had changed because food shortages became more serious. Diseases, weight loss and inadequate food forced prisoners to eat insects and wild plants. On October 20, 1944, the invasion of Leyte Island began the American invasion of the Philippines. On December 15, 1944, the invasion of Luzon had begun. On February 3, five American tanks broke through into the prison compound. The Japanese guards took 200 prisoners as hostages in the education building. During negotiations between the Americans and Japanese, one of the most hated Japanese officers, Lieutenant Abiko, reached for a grenade and was shot by one of the American soldiers. The other forty-seven Japanese soldiers were allowed to leave in return for the release of the 200 prisoners. Julia Wendt and the other prisoners were finally liberated.

On April 10, 1945, Julia again arrived at San Pedro, California, with no passport or other documents. On the forms she listed her destination as West Beach, Biloxi, Mississippi. On December 30, she was interviewed by the *Times-Picayune*. She told the reporter:

> *If I had been told that I would laugh as people spat upon and kicked a body cold in death, I would not have believed them. But I did, I laughed as I watched sick, half-starved victims of the Santo Tomas prison camp pass the ego-deflated body of the merciless camp disciplinarian, Lieutenant Abiko.*

After things in the camp had settled down, Julia, a friend and the friend's small son, who were also prisoners of war, sat down to a meal of a cup of corn meal and a can of corned beef. During their long captivity under the Japanese, her friend had hoarded the can for her young son. Now, after being liberated, they became brazen and daring, breaking the long habit of conformity and submission that had become so embedded in their minds.

Julia continued to live in Gunston Hall until about 1958. After, she continued to live in Biloxi, and from 1968 to 1981, she lived in apartment 303 in the Gulf Towers. As her health deteriorated, she moved to Lexington, Kentucky, to live with a nephew. On December 23, 1985, she died, and her remains were returned to Biloxi for burial in Southern Memorial Park.

The Mladinich family was the last family in Gunston Hall. They were the ones who converted it to the White Pillars Restaurant. Like so many Gulf Coast families of Slavonian ancestry, the Mladinich family roots come from Dalmatia. At that time, Dalmatia was part of Austria-Hungary. Giacomo Mladinich and his wife, Diana Filipic Ozurovic, had two sons—Ernest, born on September 9, 1875, and Andrew, born on October 28, 1877. Ernest Mladinich married Katherine Bonacich, and Andrew married Margaret Klemente Bonasic. Andrew and Margaret were married on January 13, 1901, in Milna. On August 6, 1902, Andrew and Margaret's son, Andrew Jake, was born in Dalmatia.

Ernest arrived at Ellis Island, New York, in 1901, and Andrew Mladinich arrived a year later. From New York, they moved to Oakland, California. They began their work in the United States in the seafood industry in California. While there is some indication that the Mladinich families moved to Biloxi in 1906, Oakland, California city directories place Andrew there in 1910–11. Since Ernest is not listed in these city directories, it is likely that he moved to Biloxi in 1906. Also in 1906, Margaret and Andrew Jake Mladinich joined Andrew in the United States.

In 1913, the two families both lived at 213 Cedar Street, and both brothers were listed as laborers. On February 18, 1915, tragedy struck Andrew's family with the death of his wife, Margaret Klemente. On July 15, 1919, Andrew married Mary Bourgeois. By 1922, Andrew lived on Cedar Street and Ernest on East Beach. By age twelve, Andrew Jake was working on a factory boat with his father and would soon just go by the name Jake.

Jake Mladinich Sr. became close friends with Mary Peirotich, who, with many of her friends, worked in the factories, too. Mary was the daughter of John Pierotich and Antonia Barhanovich. Jake continued to work with his father and had aspirations of owning his own boat. Even though the federal and state child labor laws were enacted, this did not stop the practice of child labor. In a 1970 article, Mary recalls hiding under the factory when inspectors arrived. When the inspectors had gone, they would wipe the cobwebs from their faces and return to work. There are many tales of children hiding in coal bins, ice storage, sheds and, as Mary did, under factories.

Jake's dream was fulfilled when he purchased the vessel *Winchester*. Over time, Mary became the love of Jake's life, and on June 3, 1925, Jake and Mary were married. From this union, two sons would be born, Andrew Jake and John. During the 1930s, the Mladinich family pooled their money and started the Dixie Fisheries Company. The future looked good, but disaster struck when a large amount of shrimp spoiled. This loss caused the family to close the factory, and it was eventually bought by other financiers. During these tough times, the Mladinich family returned to their roots as fishermen and factory workers.

On April 12, 1938, Andrew passed away. Jake, Mary and their two sons lived on Point Cadet. Jake Sr. continued to work in the seafood

The restored Gunston Hall, 2015. *Author's collection.*

industry, and his son Jake Jr. began working in his uncle's restaurant, the Flame, in Gulfport.

About 1949, the family made a move that would change their lives. The family bought a home on West Beach Boulevard west of Camellia Street. In 1950, they opened a restaurant and lounge called Fiesta Lounge directly south of their west beach home. In 1952, Jake and Mary were listed as owners and Jake Mladinich Jr. as manager. This was the beginning of the Mladinich family's ventures that would include the Cabana Beach Hotel, the Sea and Sirloin Restaurant, Le Chateau apartments, a coin laundry, a package liquor store, a party supply store, the Trader John Lounge and, of course, the Fiesta. Most adult Biloxi citizens can remember the Fiesta at the Fiesta sign on the west beach.

In 1966, the Mladinich family purchased Gunston Hall. The plans were to turn it into a restaurant that they would call the White Pillars. Before transformation could be completed, tragedy struck when Jake Sr. died on March 1, 1967.

Work resumed on the White Pillars, but on August 17, 1969, Hurricane Camille stormed ashore on the Mississippi Gulf. The Mladinich family found themselves, like many others, with much lost but a spirit to rebuild.

As they reconstructed their lives and businesses, work at the White Pillars started once again. The historic home was restored and redecorated using period antiques. Draperies and wallpaper were selected that best resembled the style of the nineteenth century. The White Pillars Restaurant was lit by crystal chandeliers and wall sconces, creating a special dining atmosphere. One of the centerpieces was a thirty-four-foot walnut bar with poplar trim that was installed in 1969. It was originally in the Blackstone Hotel in Chicago but was purchased by Pete Martin and installed in his Magic Door Lounge in Biloxi.

In June 1970, the White Pillars opened its doors to the public and was at once a favorite restaurant of tourist and locals. Eggplant Josephine became its signature dish. On October 1, 1983, tragedy struck the Mladinich family again with the death of Mary Pierotich Mladinich. In 1989, the family decided to close the White Pillars restaurant. It remained closed for over twenty years, but in 2008, news reports and rumors of its reopening began to surface. By midsummer of 2012, visual remodeling became the gossip. Then, on March 28, 2013, John M. Mladinich passed away before he could see his dream fulfilled. Today, there is visible progress, with finished parking lots and the restoration of Gunston Hall. Once again, we will be able to order Eggplant Josephine while dinning in the White Pillars.

12

Tullis-Toledano Manor and the Manor Families

Christoval Sebastian Toledano and his wife, Mathilde Pradat, built the Tullis-Toledano Manor and first lived there during the late 1800s. Christoval Toledano was born on August 9, 1790, in New Orleans. His father, Manuel Toledano, was born in 1763 in Fernan Nunez, Cordova, Spain. His mother was Marguerite Benoist, born in 1770 in New Orleans. Manuel and Marguerite had two other children born in New Orleans—Raphael, born in 1795, and Jerome, born in 1798.

Christoval Toledano met his first wife, Basilice Cleofas Barbay, in New Orleans. Christoval and Basilice were married on November 23, 1808, at St. Louis Cathedral in New Orleans. From this union, seven children were born. They were Clara, Dorothea, Anne, Palmyre, Benjamin, Ernest and Basilico.

In New Orleans, the young couple found themselves at the center of activities during the War of 1812. Andrew Jackson had successfully stopped the British at Pensacola and captured Pensacola on November 7. Jackson marched forces to Mobile, arriving on November 19. On November 22, Jackson's forces departed Mobile for New Orleans. In New Orleans, the men were joined by Baratarian pirates, led by Jean Lafitte; Choctaw warriors; Daquin's battalions of free men of color; and Major Jean Baptiste Plauche's Battalion d'Orleans, made up of French and Spanish gentlemen of New Orleans.

Christoval Toledano and his brothers joined Plauche's battalion. The battalion was made up of units that had existed during the French and

Spanish regimes and had been reorganized after the Louisiana Purchase. Their uniforms were based on those of the French Imperial Guard.

The British landed troops downriver from New Orleans on December 22, and Jackson counterattacked during the night of December 23. In this engagement, the British attacked the militia, thinking it was the weak point, but Plauche's and Daquin's battalions drove them back. Jackson and his troops retreated to Rodriquez Canal near Chalmette and fortified the area for the final stand. The British had eight thousand to nine thousand seasoned veterans to Andrew Jackson's roughly four thousand mixed forces. The Battle of New Orleans began on January 8, 1815. Plauche's battalion was located near the center section of Jackson's forces. After the battle, Jackson reported, "The battalion of city militia, commanded by Major Plauche realized my anticipations and behaved like veterans." Back in New Orleans, Christoval Toledano and his brothers were counted among the heroes of the Battle of New Orleans.

On September 17, 1850, Mathilde Pradat, the daughter of Pierre Pradat and Elizabeth Ixelin, purchased property in Biloxi that became the first parcel of land that would make up the Tullis-Toledano Manor. On June 25, 1856, Christoval purchased from Mathilde's brother, Louis Pradat, the section east of Mathilde's property. The front section of this parcel contained the final parcel of the Tullis-Toledano Manor. The parcel was 250 feet on the Gulf of Mexico and extended to the Biloxi Back Bay. Mathilde Pradat's and Christoval Toledano's worlds were getting ready to collide.

In 1856, Christoval was still married to Basilice Cleofas Barbay. On November 30, 1859, Basilice passed away. She was laid to rest in Lafayette Cemetery #1 in New Orleans. Her tomb reads "Basilice Barbay consort of Christoval Toledano." During this period, the word consort indicated that a woman was someone's first wife. Christoval and Mathilde's first child, Camille, was born about 1848. It is possible that Basilice and Christoval were divorced, but no records have been found. If he was divorced, it can be assumed that Christoval and Mathilde were married sometime around 1848, despite the fact that she was thirty-six years his junior.

Christoval and Mathilde would have five children. They were Camille, Rosa, Alice, John and Matilda. Alice Toledano died at the age of twelve, and John Toledano died young as well. On August 8, 1869, Christoval Toledano passed away after a lengthy illness. His remains were carried by rail to New Orleans, and he was buried in the family tomb in Lafayette Cemetery #1. The *Mobile Register* carried the story of Biloxi's *New Orleans Times*'s correspondent. The article said that another old citizen of New

Orleans had died at the age of eighty. It indicated that Christoval Toledano had served as a lieutenant at the Battle of New Orleans in Captain Plauche's company. The article reports that Biloxi was his home during the winter and summer months for many years. The article continues with his generosity to the poor who will miss him. It closes with an offering of rest in peace to the good old veteran of War of 1812.

In his will, Christoval states that Mathilde, during his illness, had taken good care of him. His will left all his property in Mississippi and Louisiana to her. His children and grandchildren, from his first marriage, filed a petition and were granted some portions of the Louisiana estate. Mathilde ended up with the largest portion of his estate. She also applied for and received a widow's pension for Christoval's service in the War of 1812.

Sometime during 1871, Mathilde sold portions of the property to Mary and Theodosia Crawford. Then in 1886, Mathilde sold the manor house and property to her niece, Carmen Valle. Mathilde then moved to Memphis, Tennessee, to be near her daughter Rosa. Rosa had married Emille LaHache, and they had one daughter, Lydia. They were later joined in Tennessee by Mathilde's son Camille. On October 20, 1902, Mathilde died in Memphis, Tennessee. She was laid to rest in the Elmwood Cemetery in Memphis.

The Tullis-Toledano Manor house. *Courtesy of the Lynn and Sandra Patterson Collection.*

What of the structures that became known as the Tullis-Toledano Manor? The manor house, the shingle house and the kitchen and servants' quarters were brick structures when built. Jean Marie Pradat was the contractor who built the Tullis-Toledano Manor between 1854 and 1855. Jean was Mathilde Pradat Toledano's uncle—her father, Pierre Pradat's, half-brother.

The Tullis-Toledano Manor main house and the servants' quarters were constructed using bricks stamped "Kendall," which meant they were from Kendall's North Biloxi Brick Yard. The stamp was not visible on the shingle house, also known as the Crawford House due to the shingled additions. The shingle house was behind and slightly east of the manor house.

The architecture of the manor house showed Greek influence, but the interior was a reflection of the early Victorian era. Most houses along the Gulf Coast were raised on piers, but Tullis-Toledano's three buildings were built on the earth level. The manor house consisted of three rooms paralleling the Mississippi Sound. The house was designed to take full advantage of cross ventilation to combat the humid weather. Additionally, the high ceilings and large attic space were imperative in keeping coastal homes cool. Initially, the middle rooms in the manor house, both upstairs and downstairs, had brick floors. The other first-floor rooms also originally had brick floors.

On the front gallery was the main staircase between floors; this allowed for more interior living space. Protruding on the manor house's east and west rear corners were closets, called cabinets. The east cabinet contained the service staircase, and the west was the service room or butler's pantry.

Originally, the reception hall in the manor house was decorated with murals. These murals were hand painted on the walls and ceiling. On the ceiling were faces showing different emotions—some jovial, some gloomy and some crazy. The east wall contained a mural of seven women in 1850s attire. The west wall showed seven gluttonous men, and the north wall had hunters in 1850s attire. Toledano family history indicates that the artist was a Frenchman named Jules LeGrand. LeGrand was a French painter of fresco murals who visited New Orleans in the late 1850s. His name also appears as a witness on one of the manor's deeds. Before Katrina, the manor house had been restored to its original magnificence.

The kitchen and servants' quarters contained a living space and a large fireplace with an oven next to it. The living quarters were on the second floor. The first-floor entrance to the staircase was on the north side of the kitchen and servants' quarters. The staircase extended up to the center of the servants' quarters to the second-floor gallery that faced the manor house. There was a brick patio beneath the gallery that extended to the brick walkway that led to the manor house. Like the manor house, the kitchen and servants' quarters were built for complete cross ventilation and with high ceilings. The first-floor rooms were built on the earth and had brick floors. The design of this structure was similar to kitchens built in New Orleans.

The shingle house had various additions over the years. In the center of this structure was the original 1850s structure. It was similar to the kitchen and servants' quarters in design but contained an archway that had been sealed. Like the manor house, the first-floor rooms were built on the earth and had brick floors. The shingle house, with its archway, was similar to the carriage houses of New Orleans. The Crawford family had enlarged the living area twice during the early 1900s. On the west side where a large oak grew, a recessed bay was built to accommodate its growth. On the south façade, a semi-octagonal bay widow was constructed, creating an appealing feature. The center structure was built for cross ventilation, but the Crawford family's additions altered this. These additions were covered with wooden shingles from the ground up, which is the reason it is called the shingle house. If the original building had remained untouched, it would have most likely been referred to as the carriage house/servants' quarters.

After a long list of owners, the final family to occupy the Tullis-Toledano Manor was the Tullis family. Garner Tullis was a successful cotton broker. (It is interesting to note that all of the Tullis-Toledano Manor families had ties to the cotton industry in New Orleans.) Tullis became the president of the New Orleans Cotton Exchange. In 1916, he married Mary Lee Brown. Tullis was also considered a renowned and competitive sailor and owned the vessel *Windjammer*. At one time, he was commodore of the Southern Yacht Club. Like so many New Orleans families, his family summered in Biloxi and wanted a summer home there.

In 1927, Mr. and Mrs. Garner Tullis purchased the shingle house and property from the Crawford family. In 1933, he acquired the parcel land east of the shingle house known as the Pool parcel. On March 25, 1939, he purchased the parcel that contained the manor house and kitchen and servants' quarters. Then, on September 30, 1939, he acquired the final parcel, which had belonged to Mathilde Pradat Toledano's sister Caroline Pradat LaHache. This reunited the properties that were once the historical structures and property of Christoval Toledano and his wife, Mathilde Pradat. The property had come full circle.

The purchasing of the manor house and kitchen and servants' quarters has some interesting aspects. In 1939, the City of Biloxi was considering turning Water Street south and connecting it to Beach Boulevard. The

A casino barge sitting on the Tullis-Toledano Manor house and Highway 90. *Author's collection.*

proposal would have Water Street running between the shingle house and the manor house. The mayor of Biloxi at that time, Louis Braun, had some concerns about this path. He telephoned Tullis and asked him if he would be interested in purchasing the manor house property. Jules Schwan, a local attorney, had already purchased it from J.B. Campbell for $5,500 in an apparent deal to resell at the same price. Of course, Tullis agreed. Both the sale from Campbell to Schwan and Schwan to Tullis were recorded in Deed Book 226, pages 141–43. Both were recorded on April 24, 1939, suggesting that they were filed concurrently.

The Tullis family's intention was to make the manor a grand summer home. They made repairs and changes to the manor house and kitchen and servants' quarters. A brick terrace and new brick walkway were installed between the manor house and kitchen and servants' quarters.

On February 18, 1966, tragedy struck the Tullis family with the death of Garner Tullis. The Tullis family continued to use the manor as a summer home. On August 10, 1969, another tragedy struck not only the manor house and kitchen and servants' quarters but also the entire

Gulf Coast—Hurricane Camille. The manor property structures were severely damaged. Mrs. Tullis decided not to repair the structures, and they remained in disrepair until 1975. Mrs. Tullis decided to sell the property "as is." She was asking $383,000 but agreed to sell the property to the City of Biloxi for $370,000. Mrs. Tullis agreed to purchase a ten-year note for $100,000 for restoration of the property. On November 9, 1975, the Tullis-Toledano Manor became the property of the City of Biloxi.

The purchase included three structures: the manor house, the shingle house, and the kitchen and servants' quarters. The three structures had been severely damaged in Hurricane Camille. Five feet of water did considerable damage on the first floor. The buildings had been vacant since the storm, but after the purchase, they were restored.

Prior to Hurricane Katrina, a huge restoration effort to restore all three structures had been completed. The restoration had returned the home to the state it was in during the Toledano era. The Tullis-Toledano Manor had become the pinnacle of historic Biloxi structures. The manor house was considered the most prominent of Biloxi's large early houses.

On August 29, 2005, Hurricane Katrina began its assault on Biloxi. The massive surge of Hurricane Katrina was too much for the three structures. The over-150-year-old bricks were no match for Katrina's battering waves. Not even the historic trees that once protected the manor were spared. A casino barge destroyed some of the trees. The barge's final insult occured when the storm surged, and wind allowed its final resting place to be on top of a portion of the manor house's foundation slab. Even though it is gone, the Tullis-Toledano Manor has not been lost to our memory or history.

13

Palmer House

Before Hurricane Camille, on the northeast corner of Seal Avenue and Central Beach Boulevard sat a large, old building. From the late 1800s to 1968, it was a boardinghouse and hotel. There is also another, little known, piece to its history—hydrotherapy was practiced at the same location. Dr. Andreas Byrenheidt, who was born in France about 1768, operated his successful hydropathic establishment in the early 1800s.

In 1852, Benjamin L. Wailes, from Natchez, had visited the Gulf Coast and recorded his visit in a journal. Wailes visited the home of Dr. Byrenheidt on August 26, 1852. He indicates that Dr. Byrenheidt had been a surgeon in Napoleon's army before migrating to Point Coupee, Louisiana. Here, Dr. Byrenheidt presented a copper coin he had recovered from his garden. The coin was marked "French Colonies 1721." We do know that in 1721 considerable quantities of nine-deniers pieces were struck in copper. They proved to be a very unpopular coin in the Americas. Many lay in storage in France while others sent to America were discarded. The good doctor owned the property from the Gulf to Biloxi Bay, so the location of his garden would be anyone's guess.

In the 1848 medical annals of Maryland, his residence is listed in New Orleans. About 1850, he relocated to Biloxi. His beachfront sanatorium was originally built as a private residence. In 1851, he was treating the daughters of William S. Hamilton of Feliciana Parish, Louisiana. Hamilton's daughter Kitty wrote to her father that she had never met a physician who had such gracefulness and thoughtfulness for the female humility. Dr. Byrenheidt

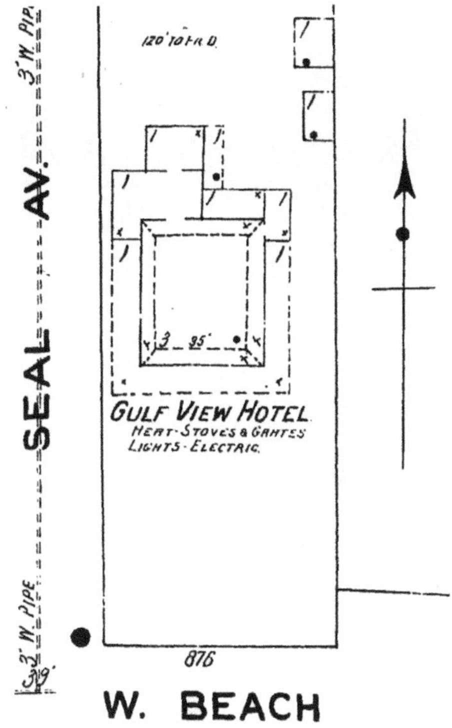

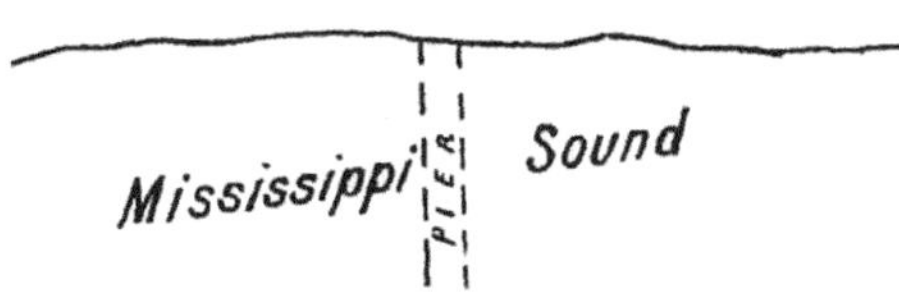

Dr. Byrenheidt's home when it was the Gulf View Hotel Sanborn on a 1909 map. *Author's collection.*

indicated that her illness was a mixture of two acids in her blood but that she could be cured by water treatment. Her sister, Penelope, indicated that she wished she had gone to Dr. Byrenheidt sooner instead of the pill givers. She wrote that it was a joyful transformation from toxic drugs to pure, cold water.

What Penelope was alluding to was the use of opiates and calomel by the medical communities in the early 1800s. Of course, opiates were highly addictive, and calomel was potentially lethal. Doctors distributed these drugs with little if any regard to the side effects. The external and internal use of water cure most likely did clean the body of these drugs. The treatment consisted of cold-water bathing, wet bandages and cold-water enemas. Dr. Byrenheidt used Biloxi's artisan water that he deemed good for one's health. He also incorporated the use of dumbbells, skipping rope and other exercises. Dr. Byrenheidt's sanatorium attracted the elite of New Orleans and was considered a form of health tourism.

In 1853, yellow fever visited the Gulf Coast. At his Biloxi establishment, Dr. Byrenheidt treated and reported 533 cases. Biloxi's population was over five thousand, and 111 deaths were reported by the good doctor at Biloxi during this outbreak. On March 4, 1859, Dr. Byrenheidt died and was laid to rest in the Biloxi Cemetery.

After his death, his business was converted into the Gulf View Hotel. In 1888, Peter J. Montross, a native of New Orleans and the owner of

Colonel Apperson's Memphis Hotel. *Courtesy of the Maritime and Seafood Industry Museum.*

the Montross Hotel, leased and managed the Gulf View Hotel. Montross passed away on March 27, 1897. The property may have been held in estate for some time, but George W. Wilkes of Indiana eventually purchased the Gulf View Hotel and surrounding property. He continued to operate it as the Gulf View Hotel. In 1910, George W. Wilkes; his wife, Laura; and three of their children resided at 776 West Beach Boulevard. Of course, the Wilkes name is familiar to locals as the name of the founder of the *Biloxi Daily Herald*.

The Wilkes family lived on West Beach Boulevard until about 1913, when Colonel John W. Apperson converted it into the Memphis Hotel. The Memphis was basically a boardinghouse styled like a hotel. Colonel Apperson's name should also be familiar because, in 1924, he would become the manager of the new Buena Vista Hotel and would be one of the investors in the Ile of Caprice gambling resort in 1925.

Long before taking over the reins of the Buena Vista, Colonel Apperson became manager of the Montross Hotel. He sold the Memphis to John S. Hord, a Mississippi planter. John and his wife, Virginia, built a home nearby at 872 West Beach Boulevard. Hord sold the Memphis to the Palmer family before 1920. In the 1920 census, Charles Palmer; his wife, Mary; and daughter, Elizabeth, are listed at 776 West Beach Boulevard.

The Palmer House Hotel. *Courtesy of the Alan Santa Cruz Collection.*

The Palmer family was originally from Connecticut but had moved to Chicago, Illinois, before 1900. On August 9, 1922, Charles Palmer passed away and was buried in the Biloxi Cemetery. Elizabeth and her mother continued to live at 776 West Beach. Elizabeth remained unmarried for the rest of her life. In 1922, she was listed as the owner of the Hotel Palmer. Elizabeth had renamed the old Memphis Hotel the Hotel Palmer, and it would remain so until 1936. On September 16, 1936, Elizabeth passed away. That year, the hotel was renamed the Palmer House and was being managed by Gertrude Warren. In 1938, Mary Palmer passed away.

Absalom Jackson and his wife, Willie—both of Alabama—had been running a boardinghouse in Biloxi. They purchased the Palmer House, and by 1949, the Jacksons had also acquired the Palms Hotel on West Beach. On August 22, 1959, Absalom passed away and was buried in the Oakwood Cemetery in Montgomery, Alabama. In 1968, the Palmer House ceased to function as a hotel. Then on August 17, 1969, Hurricane Camille struck, destroying many homes along Biloxi's shoreline, including the Palmer Hotel.

14

Edgewater Gulf Hotel

A lot of folks remember the Edgewater Gulf Hotel standing tall just east of the Edgewater Mall. Unfortunately, the Edgewater Mall's expansion in 1971 marked the end of the forty-four-year legacy of this grand hotel.

On August 2, 1925, the *Times-Picayune* reported that a big hotel would be opening by Christmas 1926. The architect was Benjamin H. Marshall of Chicago. The hotel was to be built between Biloxi and Gulfport. The building was originally set to go in an area with beautiful, giant oaks. Marshall decided to build it nearer to the beach to save the large oaks. It was noted that the Old Belmar Hotel was on this new location. The developers had determined that nature would be taken into partnership in the development of the Edgewater Gulf site and that the talented architect would have free rein. These Chicago investors were the owners of the Edgewater Beach Hotel in Chicago.

The investors felt the new hotel created a new resort era along the Mississippi Gulf Coast. In 1926, there were three grand hotels under construction. The Pine Hills Hotel was being built on the north shore of the Bay of St. Louis. The eight-story Hotel Markham was under construction in downtown Gulfport, and the Edgewater Gulf Hotel was taking shape in Biloxi. Additionally, there were plans for the Gulf Hills Resort on Biloxi Bay in Jackson County and the Isles on Bay of St. Louis in Pass Christian. Due to construction and weather delays, the opening of the Edgewater Gulf Hotel was set for January 10, 1927.

The new $2.5 million hotel was ten stories high with a fourteen-story tower in the center. There were four hundred rooms, all facing the water,

An aerial view of the Edgewater Gulf Hotel and grounds. *Courtesy of the Alan Santa Cruz Collection.*

The Edgewater Gulf Hotel swimming pool full of hotel guests. *Courtesy of the Alan Santa Cruz Collection.*

to accommodate visiting tourists. The hotel building also incorporated a parking garage, a concept first introduced by the Edgewater Beach Hotel in Chicago. The hotel's outside dancing pavilion, riding stables with twenty horses, swimming pools, boat and fishing trips, tennis courts, gardens and eighteen-hole golf course were available to the hotel's guests. In addition to ballrooms, there was a main dining room and the sun dining room.

The tourist market in Illinois was the target of the Edgewater Gulf Hotel. For the grand opening, a special Illinois Central Railroad train ran from Chicago to Gulfport for the winter season. By August 1926, early reservations for the opening from St. Louis, Missouri, caused the addition of an extra passenger coach and an unplanned stop in St. Louis. In October, the Illinois Central Railroad added an additional train, and by January 1, 1927, special trains transported 1,100 guests. Hotel guests traveled the new paved driveway from the Louisville and Nashville (L&N) train station to the lobby of the hotel. Also, the Oriole Terrace Orchestra from the Edgewater Beach Hotel in Chicago was on hand for the grand opening and the winter season.

On January 9, 1927, the new Edgewater Gulf Hotel was turned over to the hotel management. The average size of the hotel rooms was nineteen

The sun porch facing the Mississippi Sound. *Courtesy of the Alan Santa Cruz Collection.*

by twenty-five feet with at least two windows, but the majority had three windows. The Edgewater Gulf was the first hotel to claim that all its rooms faced the water of the Mississippi Sound.

On January 10, 1927, a crowd of over 1,000 guests attended the grand opening of the Edgewater Gulf Hotel. The second-floor lobby, lounge, dining room and ballroom were arranged into one great room that could have accommodated 2,500 guests.

It was reported that the dining room should be referred to as the "dining porch." Most likely, it was the only entirely glassed-in dining room in America. The dining room faced the Mississippi Sound and ran the length of the building. For the summer months, canopies protected diners from the sun and inclement weather. In addition, a glassed-in swimming pool would be available during the winter months. The large, circular fireplace was the main feature in the lobby that made it resemble a palace. The fireplace was advertised as being able to lodge eight groups at one time, doing away with people packing around one fireplace.

The ground floor of the hotel was filled with shops and a commissary for use by hotel guests and residents of Edgewater Park. This residential subdivision was located east and north of the Edgewater Gulf Hotel and was developed by the hotel's investors.

The large, circular grand fire place in the Edgewater Gulf Hotel lobby. *Courtesy of the Lynn and Sandra Patterson Collection.*

Edgewater Gulf Hotel. *Courtesy of the Alan Santa Cruz Collection.*

William M. Dewey of Chicago was appointed managing director of the new hotel. Tommy Burns and W.W. Myers were the resident managers. Meyer Eiseman, a New Orleans realtor, and J.W. Billings, a New Orleans engineer, greeted entrepreneurs of the Midwest. Eiseman said the hotel would be the forerunner of other beachfront projects on the Mississippi Gulf Coast. Another New Orleans entrepreneur, Leon Simon, indicated that people in New Orleans believed that the Mississippi coast was an ideal tourist area and nothing would entertain them better than to see the Gulf Coast developed into one of the greatest all-year resorts in America.

The hotel fell on bad times during the Great Depression, and in 1932, a Chicago bank filed suit to foreclose and won. The Edgewater Gulf Hotel changed owners many times and had many ups and downs during its forty-four years. Through the years, many loyal patrons returned time and time again. Finally, in February 1971, its new owners, the American National Insurance Company, decided to demolish the grand old hotel.

On July 25, 1971, a demolition team was set to send the grand old hotel to the ground. The blasts thundered through the rooms. As the smoke cleared, it was obvious the old hotel was not going out without a fight. The west and east wings were still standing. Mark Loizeaux, the chief of Controlled Demolition Incorporated of Maryland, stated he would love to meet the guy who designed it. He concluded that it was not only an admirable but also as formidable structure. In the days that followed, the hotel received its last bow and faded into history.

15

Avelez Hotel

In early 1923 Biloxi, there was talk of construction of the new five-story Avelez Hotel. The new hotel would be constructed in downtown Biloxi. The five-story hotel would face Howard Avenue between Magnolia and Croesus Streets. The building was originally designed with an arcade entrance centered in the middle of the block and flanked by shops on both sides. The *Daily Herald* indicated that the five-story hotel would have the latest innovations.

Each of the one hundred rooms in the Avelez Hotel would have a connecting bath. Today, we would be shocked to find our hotel room did not have a bathroom. In 1923, the bathrooms in older hotels were usually public baths, and if you were lucky, they were just down the hall. Of course, if you ever travel to Europe, make sure your room has a connecting bath. It is quite common in some hotels to share bathrooms. The bathrooms in the Avelez also would have tile flooring, direct flushing sanitary fixtures and hot and cold running water.

In addition to a connecting bath, each room was to be furnished with modern furniture, including mattresses made of the best box spring design and manufactured by Simmons Hardware Company of St. Louis, Missouri. The doors, according to the article, were ventilating doors and were considered indestructible. The hotel would be steam heated by a boiler and have electrical lighting. As construction continued, the grand opening of the Avelez Hotel was scheduled for New Year's Eve 1923.

The manager for the Avelez was Phil C. Caldwell. Caldwell was an experienced hotel man. He had been manager at the Great Southern

The Avelez Hotel with stores in the front, 1923. *Courtesy of the Alan Santa Cruz Collection.*

The Avelez Hotel, 1920s. *Courtesy of the Alan Santa Cruz Collection.*

Hotel in Gulfport; the Hotel Galvez in Galveston, Texas; and the Hotel Hattiesburg in Hattiesburg, Mississippi. It appears that Caldwell enticed some of his employees in Hattiesburg to journey with him to Biloxi. The additional workers who completed his workforce hailed from Biloxi.

In December, the staff worked day and night to have the building ready to open. On December 28, a half-page invitation to the people of the Mississippi coast was posted in the *Daily Herald*. On December 31, the *Daily Herald* reported that the work on the Avelez Hotel building was not totally completed. The report indicated that enough was completed to open one floor to hotel guests. The lobby and arcade were also completed and would be the setting of the New Year's Eve grand opening and dance. A tour of the whole structure was promised to all who attended the opening. Two rooms on the completed floor were set aside for the tours, and all the rest had been booked by visitors. Some of the visitors were Mr. and Mrs. A. Mac Jones, Mr. and Mrs. C.M. Willoughby, W.E. Harmon, Francis Deas and Mr. and Mrs. Allen from Hattiesburg.

On New Year's Eve 1923, the Avelez held a grand opening that was attended by hundreds. Manager Phil Caldwell and his wife—as well as his management assistants, Mr. and Mrs. Edward Brady—were in the receiving line.

The Avelez Hotel, 1930s. *Courtesy of the Lynn and Sandra Patterson Collection.*

The Avelez Hotel. *Courtesy of the Lynn and Sandra Patterson Collection.*

Guests entered the hotel through a spacious arcade that led to one of the largest hotel lobbies along the Gulf Coast. Those who wanted to tour the completed guest rooms rode the eight-person elevator to the fifth floor. There, Mrs. M.C. Pankey—the head of housekeeping and a Hattiesburg native—conducted the tours. Two rooms were left vacant for the tours while guests occupied the rest of the twenty-five completed rooms. Hotel guests and those attending the opening came from Biloxi, Gulfport, Laurel, Hattiesburg and other Gulf Coast communities. The carpeted floors, electrical lighting, steam heating and the other accommodations that were offered became the subject of the evening.

Later in the evening, music by the All Southern Syncopators filled the lobby and arcade. Punch was served, and favors in the form of balloons were distributed to the guests. Many guests stayed into the wee hours, dancing the old year out and the New Year in.

Telegrams congratulating Caldwell arrived from other hotel managers. Some messages came from James Lynch, Hotel De Soto, New Orleans; George Stearge, Hotel Hattiesburg, Hattiesburg, Mississippi; N.D., West Aleazar, Clarksdale, Mississippi; Harry Halfnero, Portage Hotel, Akron, Ohio; and Phillip Toulme, a Hattiesburg businessman.

It was noted that the opening of Biloxi's beautiful hotel was in keeping with the growth of the city. Some of the shops located in the Avelez were a barbershop, a beauty shop, a cigar stand, cafés, a restaurant and the Avelez Lounge.

In 1936, R.C. Allen operated the barbershop, Mrs. Stevius Manios ran the café, Virginia Abrams managed the cigar stand and J.L. Betancourt was the manager. During the late 1940s, Salvatore and Josephine Sicuro operated the lounge. In 1949, J.E. and Esther Johnston operated the lounge.

The Avelez continued operating as the Avelez, but between 1946 and 1949, it was purchased and renamed the Earle Hotel. Hotel founder Earle Reid Milner opened his first hotel, the Milner Hotel, in Detroit. His successful hotel business expanded across the United States. Milner Hotel Inc. opened various hotels as the Milner and Earle Hotels and continues as a business to this day. The Milner Hotel Inc. Biloxi venue was short lived.

Sometime between 1954 and 1958, the Earle was renamed the New Avelez Hotel. The new manager was Richard E. Basile. In 1967, the New Avelez Hotel closed its doors for good, and the structure gave way to progress.

16
Tivoli Hotel

During the aftermath of Katrina, Biloxians let their lives fall into an almost ritual mode. They went about their lives numb to their surroundings. The sounds of hurricane-destroyed homes and businesses being removed by heavy equipment and hauled away by any type of vehicle available became a normal occurrence. Gradually, most of these sounds died away and were replaced by the sounds of hammers, power tools and other construction equipment. The recovery has been very slow but, for the most part, positive.

One morning, I was working and was kind of enjoying the birds singing in the nearby trees and the relative quiet of that morning. Then, I realized that in the background I could hear the sound of heavy equipment moving on its tracks as it worked itself into position and then quiet again; the equipment had stopped. The quiet was short lived because the next sound I heard was a heavy object striking something solid. The solid object had not held though, and the next sound was like hundreds of thousands of pieces of glass showering to the ground. It didn't take me long to realize that the sound was a wrecking ball striking the Tivoli Hotel. What had sounded like glass were the shattered pieces of brick raining down the sides of the hotel to the ground. The once grand Tivoli had been the product of the 1920s, and like many of its sister hotels from the same period, its physical history was coming to an end.

During the mid-1920s, the Mississippi Gulf Coast was referred to as the American Riviera of the South. Some of the older hotels had been

An artist's rendition of the Tivoli Hotel, circa 1927. *Courtesy of the Alan Santa Cruz Collection.*

remodeled magnificently while newer ones—like the Pine Hills Hotel in Bay St. Louis, the Markham Hotel in Gulfport and the Gulf Hills Hotel in Ocean Springs—were being built. The years between 1925 and 1927 saw the construction of five new hotels in Biloxi. They were the Buena Vista, the Avelez, the Tivoli, the New Biloxi and the Edgewater Gulf Hotel. When the Tivoli Hotel opened its doors, its rooms were referred to as apartments. It had twenty-four two- and three-room apartments for its guests and sixty-four regular hotel rooms. The four-floored Tivoli stood tall and proud among the huge oaks that lined Biloxi's East Beach. The lobby was built with a barrel-style vaulted ceiling with a grand ballroom on one side and a large dining room on the other.

The Tivoli's grand opening occurred on February 19, 1927. During the grand opening, the jazz band could be heard for blocks as one neared the hotel. Thousands of lights reflected off the shimmering walls. Three hundred dignitaries and locals danced the night away in the colorfully lit ballroom. The Roaring Twenties had arrived along the Mississippi Gulf Coast.

The Tivoli, like many other popular Biloxi beach resorts, offered golfing, motoring, relaxing, fishing, tennis and boating. Another form of entertainment was gambling, which was quite visible in the form of slot

The Tivoli Hotel, 1950s. *Courtesy of the Becky Rose Collection.*

The Tivoli Hotel when it was the Trade Winds Hotel. *Courtesy of the Alan Santa Cruz Collection.*

machines that could be found in many hotels—the Pine Hills in Bay St. Louis and the Edgewater Gulf, the Buena Vista, the White House and, of course, the Tivoli in Biloxi. In fact, at that time, slot machines could be found in grocery stores and other businesses along the Mississippi Gulf Coast.

In 1927, excellent business was reported by Biloxi hotels, including the Edgewater Gulf Hotel, the White House Hotel, the Riviera Hotel, the Buena Vista Biloxi Hotel, the Kennedy Hotel, the Park Hotel, the Avelez Hotel and the Tivoli Hotel. In 1929, a writer touring the Spanish Trail indicated that when he arrived in Biloxi, he asked a citizen which hotel was regarded as the finest. The citizen replied, "Why, the Tivoli." The influx of northern patrons boosted the hotel industry for many years, but with changing times, the industry began to falter. In October 1929, the stock market crashed and was followed by the Great Depression. Like many hotels, the Tivoli found itself in financial troubles.

The Tivoli changed owners and become known as the Trade Winds Hotel until about 1969. I remember swimming and diving off the Trade Winds pier. It didn't take us Point kids long to realize we could swim in the Trade Winds pool by sneaking in the east side door of the lobby. Once inside, we would look for a female guest headed for the pool and walk just behind her and enter the pool area. Every now and again, a new lifeguard would catch us, but we would be at it again in a day or two. One thing I noticed

On the left, a casino barge laying across the Tivoli Hotel property and against the hotel. *Author's collection.*

during these visits was how grand the lobby was. It was like something I had never seen before. It had very ornate gold trim, and I can only imagine that when it was new, it truly must have been grand. As young adults, we would often go to the lounge in the Tivoli where we could have drinks and dance the night away. I remember sitting in the old lobby and seeing its former grandeur still showing under faded paint and dust.

In later years, the Tivoli name was restored. After a long use as rental apartments, the Tivoli sat vacant for many years. The Biloxi Yacht Club moved into the Trade Winds office, bar and pool area of the property while the Tivoli sat in the background. During this time, investors talked of restoring the Tivoli as a hotel or health center while others researched some other uses. But the building remained an empty shell waiting to be restored to its former glory. The hotel itself was in need of a huge restoration, but a ray of hope appeared in 2003 when it was added to the Ten Most Endangered Historical Places in Mississippi list. There was hope that it could be restored and returned to it 1920s glory, but on August 29, Hurricane Katrina landed the final blows that led to its demise at the end of a wrecking ball.

17

White House Hotel

For many years, while driving along Highway 90 in Biloxi, no one could help noticing the large, empty shell of a building at the corner of Highway 90 and White Avenue. Longtime Coastians know that this empty shell was once the elegant White House Hotel. The old White House Hotel has been in the news lately, and while some news has been negative, the more recent news sounds promising for restoration.

Walter A. White and his wife, Cora Inez Enoch, were the White House Hotel originators and owners. Walter A. White was born on Steen's Creek near Brandon, Mississippi, on December 1, 1854. His parents were Thomas S. White and Selina Caroline Cooper. Cora Inez Enoch was born in nearby Terry, in Hinds County, Mississippi, on January 27, 1864, to Captain Isaac V. Enoch and Julia Harriett Byrd. She also had an older sister, Julia Harriett Enoch.

Walter White went to school in Rankin County, and after graduating, he studied law under the influences of some very powerful Mississippians. Around 1873, he studied law under the direction of Anselm J. McLaurin in Brandon. McLaurin had fought with the Third Mississippi Artillery during the Civil War. After the war, he opened a practice in Smith County but returned to Brandon in 1872. In 1896, McLaurin would be elected the thirty-fourth governor of Mississippi.

While studying law and working under McLaurin, White met and married Julia Harriet Enoch on February 15, 1877. From this union, he would have four daughters: Cora, Lula, Laura and Nell. In 1882, White teamed up with Colonel H.S. Cole and formed the law firm of Cole & White.

The White family home on Beach Road, Biloxi, circa 1894. *Courtesy of the Maritime and Seafood Industry Museum.*

Around 1887, tragedy struck with the death of Walter White's beloved wife and mother of his children, Julia Harriet White. In 1889, roughly two years after Julia's death, Walter White married Julia's younger sister, Cora Inez Enoch. The same year, whether for business or pleasure, Walter White visited the Biloxi area. While on the coast, he stayed in the Beauvoir community. By 1890, he left the firm of Cole & White and moved his family to the Beauvoir community. On April 12, 1890, he moved his law practice from Beauvoir to Biloxi.

In Biloxi, he opened his law office on the south side of Pass Christian Road (today's Howard Avenue) between Lameuse and Main Streets. For some time, the Whites lived in the Mexican Gulf Hotel, known to most as the Palmer House. In 1891, Cora gave birth to their first child, Walter Enoch White. Around 1892, they moved to Magnolia Street, but by 1894, they had moved again into a new home on Biloxi Beach. Eventually, this was the location of the White House Hotel. This same year, Judge James H. Neville joined Walter in his law firm. Judge Neville had been the district

Four of the homes that would make up the White House Hotel. *Courtesy of the Alan Santa Cruz Collection. Inset*: Cora Enochs White. *Courtesy of Bettie Fore.*

attorney for twelve years. In 1896, Judge Neville resigned as district attorney, and Governor McLaurin, White's former teacher, appointed him district attorney of Harrison County, Mississippi. This appointment led to his circuit court judgeship in 1925.

Sometime after 1892, Walter and Cora White lost an infant son, and in 1899, Harry White, another young son, passed away. While life appeared bleak for the couple, the fortune of the White family was about to change. According to White family history, sometime in 1899, Cora began to take boarders into the White home. In 1901, Cora again gave birth to a son, John G. White. By 1903, the White family had purchased large tracts of land and some large houses, launching the family into the hotel business.

In 1906, the White House advertised for the first time in the *Daily Herald*. The ad read:

> *The White House west end beach, Biloxi, Miss. Beautiful large grounds on the beach and electric car line, boating, fishing, good food, good beds, modern conveniences. Cottages for families make the accommodations ideal for the seashore, rates, $8 to $12 per week Mrs. Cora E. White proprietress.*

The White House Hotel with the 1912 additions by architect T.J. Rosell. *Courtesy of the Alan Santa Cruz Collection.*

By 1908, there were six White homes in the White House Hotel complex. Mrs. White recognized that Biloxi could develop into a winter resort for northern visitors. By 1912, the Whites had acquired nine large houses along Biloxi Beach. The same year, extensive improvements were made to the White House Hotel complex. Architect T.J. Rosell was hired to make the improvements. Rosell added a central building that connected two of the large houses. This new building had a beautiful lobby and a 150-foot-long porch overlooking the gulf. A 40- by 96-foot dining room was added off the spacious lobby. The central building was three stories high and contained forty hotel rooms. All of these rooms boasted electric lighting, steam heating and hot and cold running water with modern lavatories. With thirty-two baths, many of the rooms had private baths, while the rest had a bath shared with another room. The White House had become a first-class hotel.

In addition to all the improvements to the White House, 1912 was a very active year. Mrs. White had a booklet printed that promoted Biloxi as a summer and winter resort. The booklet was distributed to patrons all over the nation. Just north of the hotel, the White House had its own farm, with vegetable gardens, hogs, chickens and a dairy to provide fresh food and drink for it patrons and the citizens of Biloxi. On April 3, 1912, Mrs. White purchased the McDonald and Pirie Dairies. The White

Right: Judge Walter White sitting on the White House fountain. *Courtesy of Bettie Fore.*

Below: The White House's groundbreaking ceremony for the 1928 expansion. *Left to right*: Walter E. White, U.S. senator Pat Harrison, Judge Walter White, architect George B. Rogers and John T. White. *Courtesy of Bettie Fore.*

House now owned seventy-five acres of land on Pass Road, stretching from the Naval Reverse Park (Keesler Air Force Base) to present-day McDonald Avenue.

In a male-oriented society, Mrs. White became a leader in the tourism industry, a visionary for the future of Biloxi and the initiator of the White House Hotel Company. Judge Walter White's success in the Mississippi judicial system and Cora White's success in tourism made the couple a prevailing presence in the business and social community of the Gulf Coast and the state of Mississippi.

For almost three decades, the White House Hotel was very successful. In 1926, Cora turned over the management of the White House to her sons John T. and Walter White, but her presence and influence on the daily operation of the hotel continued.

In the late 1920s, the Mississippi Gulf Coast saw a surge in tourism and new hotel construction. The White brothers knew how important it was to keep up with the competition. Improvements were made in 1927, and beginning in July 1929, a large expansion occurred. The four-story 1929 addition was added to the east side of the hotel complex. An observation tower crowned the fifth floor. Using Colonial-style architecture, the block structure was advertised as completely fireproof. This final addition added fifty new rooms, bringing the White House total to 168 rooms. The other buildings were also being remodeled to conform to the Colonial style of the new building. The addition gave the White House a competitive advantage because it now had the space to host conventions. The convention auditorium had a view of the Mississippi Sound, and White House patrons attended many dances there.

On October 29, 1929, the stock market crash marked the beginning of the Great Depression. Many of the Gulf Coast hotels became bankrupt and changed hands many times. The White House struggled but persevered under John and Walter White. About 1932, John became the sole manager of the White House Hotel when his brother Walter left the hotel business for the insurance business.

On September 9, 1934, tragedy struck the family with the death of Cora White. One of the notes in her obituary states that her death had removed from Biloxi one of the most important female citizens of the community and state. It also stated that Judge and Mrs. White had raised twenty children—their own, nieces, nephews and a few orphans. Above and beyond her public service, Cora showed a lot of kindness to her friends, relatives and neighbors.

The White House Hotel, 2015. *Author's collection. Inset*: Cora Enoch White. *Courtesy of Bettie Fore.*

In 1940, after forty years in the hotel business, the White family sold the White House Hotel to the Love family. The Love family now owned the Buena Vista and the White House Hotel. Two short years later, Judge Walter White passed away on April 8, 1942. Judge White was living just a short distance from his beloved White House Hotel on Morrison Avenue. From 1896 until 1904, Judge White had served as district attorney. He had also served as circuit court judge from 1925 to 1939 before retiring. For over forty years, the White family had influenced the Mississippi judicial system, as well as the business and the social communities of the Mississippi Gulf Coast. Once again, we are seeing the fruits of their labor in the restored White House Hotel.

18

Magnolia Hotel

Queen of the Watering Holes

The Magnolia Hotel is not a functioning hotel, but it is the oldest existing antebellum hotel along the Mississippi Gulf Coast. Severely wounded by Katrina, this was not the first time a hurricane had damaged it. The sturdily built Magnolia Hotel has a long history in Biloxi, but it is also a standing tribute to the long history of tourism along the Mississippi Gulf Coast.

For many years, the Mississippi Gulf Coast was considered a perfect place for health and relaxation and the rejuvenation of one's body. Between 1817 and 1860, Biloxi began to slowly develop from a primitive area into a favorite summer resort place for many southerners. In 1838, Biloxi was incorporated as a township.

John Hahn built the Magnolia Hotel in 1847. John Hahn's name also appears as John Hohn in some local records. Who was John Hahn? Written accounts indicate that he arrived in the United States as a minor in 1829 from Hanover, Germany. Some records indicate he was a saloonkeeper in New Orleans, and in 1842, he is listed as owning a coffeehouse at 246 Front Levee Street.

When Hahn arrived in Biloxi is unknown, but there is one story that indicates the reason he moved to Biloxi was that his son had become seriously ill. A doctor in New Orleans recommended the child would fare better on the Mississippi Gulf Coast. John relocated his family to Biloxi, and the boy's health improved. Due to the child's recovery, John decided to make Biloxi the family's home.

Left: The Magnolia Hotel before 1969. *Courtesy of the Maritime and Seafood Industry Museum.*

Below: The Magnolia Hotel after 1969. *Courtesy of the Lynn and Sandra Patterson Collection.*

On March 23, 1847, John Hahn entered into a contract with Charles Kaufman to build a two-story frame house. The structure was located near and faced the beach. It was forty square feet and had a seven-foot-wide gallery wrapping around the first and second stories. There was a chimney that ran from the ground floor to the roof and connected two fireplaces. Construction on the Magnolia Hotel was completed in late 1847, and rumor said it was named for a large magnolia tree located on the property.

Some written accounts indicate that John Hahn tended bar in the Magnolia Hotel and died within a year of its construction. There are also conflicting accounts of his death, which some records indicate occurred on April 4, 1848. While Biloxi Cemetery records indicate that John Hahn, who was born in 1806, died in 1847, his estate was inventoried in 1848, and it is possible that the settlement on the estate was in 1848 while his death was in late 1847.

We do know that his widow, Elizabeth Hahn, petitioned the probate court for full control of his estate. The court ruled in her favor, and Elizabeth Hahn took sole control of the Magnolia Hotel and gradually paid off all debtors.

Before the Civil War, tourism began in earnest when many wealthy plantation owners—from Mississippi, Alabama and Louisiana—as well as wealthy citizens of New Orleans, began to visit the Mississippi Gulf Coast on an annual basis.

New Orleans's citizens traveled to Biloxi and the Mississippi coast in hopes of escaping the yellow fever epidemics. Many of New Orleans's wealthy built large waterfront homes and traveled by steamboat to Biloxi, bringing entire households and servants. Plantation owners from Mississippi, Alabama and Louisiana built summer homes on the coast as well.

By late 1850, Biloxi had several fine hotels, or watering places, as they were called. They included the Magnolia Hotel, the American Hotel, the Biloxi House, the Green Oaks Hotel and the Shady Oaks Hotel, as well as many fine boardinghouses. The attics of many of these hotels were made into large rooms used as common sleeping dorms or bachelor quarters for single, young men.

One of the essential elements of these hotels was the galleries. Most hotels had no interior hall, which meant hotel rooms had to be accessed from the galleries. These galleries became the area for social events and relaxation.

Mrs. Hahn did a good job of managing the Magnolia, and during the 1850s, it was considered one of the favorite hotels on the coast. During the 1880s, the Magnolia Hotel was one of the most popular hotels due to its location near the steamer piers. In later years, it was popular for being a reasonable distance from the railroad. Its location near the beach was another reason it was so popular. The cost for a room plus meals averaged around thirty-five dollars a month, ten dollars a week or two dollars a day. Of course, children and servants were half price. Along the Magnolia Hotel's beachfront, one could fish, use one of the pleasure boats, bowl in the ten-pin alley or just relax at the bar.

In the years after the Civil War, many hotels along the Mississippi Gulf Coast struggled or closed. Their salvation came in the form of the iron horse in 1869. In due time, visitors began to come by train from Midwestern and northern states to escape harsh winters. Because there were so many visitors from New Orleans, the Louisville and Nashville Railroad ran excursions twice a week to accommodate them. These special excursions, which would run two or three times a day, began in the spring and ended in late fall.

Local hotels like the Magnolia Hotel began to cater to both the snowbirds and the New Orleanians. Mrs. Hahn began to offer these excursion guests a bath and dinner for seventy-five cents. Soon a decision was made to build a large wing west of the Magnolia Hotel to house a dining room and kitchen. This would allow room for accommodations for both overnight and day excursion guests. The larger kitchen and dining hall was soon used by locals and guests for New Year's Eve celebrations, Mardi Gras balls and the volunteer fire companies' balls.

The Magnolia Hotel weathered numerous hurricanes. One was the August 26, 1860 storm, which records indicate rose to the top of the porch banister and beat against the wall. In 1893, the Magnolia Hotel even hosted

The Magnolia Hotel after Hurricane Katrina in 2005. *Author's collection.*

The Magnolia Hotel, home of the Mardi Gras Museum, 2015. *Author's collection.*

two Australian prizefighters who were scheduled to box two fighters from the New Orleans Olympics Club. Joe Goddard and George Dawson trained along the Mississippi Gulf Coast from late January to early March 1893. How successful they were is unknown, but during their stay, they made many friends along the coast.

Tragedy struck the Hahn family on October 5, 1904, with the passing of Elizabeth. Her daughter and son continued to run the Magnolia Hotel. By the early 1900s, tourism along the coast had set the stage for change. Investors looking to capitalize on the growth began to invest in large hotel developments. These developments during the 1920s were the Pine Hill Hotel Bay in St. Louis, the Markham in Gulfport, the Gulf Hills in Ocean Springs, the Buena Vista, the Avelez, the Tivoli, the New Biloxi and the Edgewater Hotels in Biloxi. These new hotels joined the ranks with some of the veteran hotels like the White House, the Riviera, the Kennedy and the Park Hotels.

The boardinghouses and small hotels began to suffer, and the Magnolia was no exception. Its use as a hotel ended around 1941. The future of the old structure didn't look promising. On August 17, 1969, Hurricane Camille slammed into the Mississippi Gulf Coast. The Magnolia Hotel was extensively damaged. At first look, it appeared that the Queen of the Watering Holes (as the Magnolia was called) was beyond repair. The porch flooring had washed away, and there were other repairs to be made. While in this state of disrepair, the hand-hewn timbers were visible. This solid construction was the reason the Magnolia had survived while other structures disintegrated around it. Under the leadership of Glenn Swetman, a group of concerned individuals got together and began to raise money for repairs. The Magnolia was moved about 150 yards north of its original site and turned to face east on the Rue Magnolia Walking Mall. Here, it was used by numerous organizations like the Biloxi Art Association, the Gulf Coast Dance Theatre and the Gulf Coast Carnival Association. In the 1990s, it was transformed into the Mardi Gras Museum until the museum was moved to the Dantzler House in 2005.

That same year, Hurricane Katrina slammed into the coast, and the Magnolia Hotel was once more damaged by a major storm. One blessing is that the 1969 move lessened the blow of Katrina. Although it was heavily damaged, the Magnolia was restored to its former glory. Today, it once again houses the Mardi Gras Museum. Listed on the National Register of Historic Places, it is truly one of our historic treasurers, and its restoration will benefit many generations to come.

19

Baricev's Seafood Harbor Restaurant and Lounge

The advertisement for Baricev's Seafood Harbor Restaurant and Lounge lists oysters on the half shell, boiled shrimp, stuffed flounder and delicious Creole seafood gumbo. It makes your mouth water just thinking about it. From 1949 to 1993, Baricev's was a must-eat place for locals and tourists alike.

The first generation of Baricevs arrived about 1914, coming through Ellis Island to Biloxi. Petar Marion Baricev and Tereza Buljacic were both born in 1880 in Molat, Dalmatia, Austria, present-day Croatia. In 1902, Petar and Tereza married in Austria. Three of their five children—John, Joseph P. and Anthony—were born in Austria, while Peter and Josephine were born in Biloxi. Here, the Baricev family, like many other Slavonian immigrants, went to work in the seafood factories and on the boats. In 1922, John and his father were listed as fishermen and, with Joseph, lived at 427 Crawford Street.

Somewhere around 1922, Joseph P. Baricev relocated to New Orleans. Here, he worked as an auto mechanic and in various restaurants. While in New Orleans, he met Jessie Traina, the daughter of Biaggio Traina and Victoria Mustacchia, both immigrants from Italy. Jessie's father, Biaggio, had died in 1904. Their engagement was announced in the *New Orleans Times-Picayune* on October 11, 1925, and they later married in New Orleans.

By 1930, Joseph P. was operating his own restaurant, called the Auditorium Restaurant at 700 North Rampart Street. His brother, Peter, was employed as the Auditorium's cook. On May 27, 1934, the *Times-*

Baricev's Seafood Harbor Restaurant and Lounge, 1940s. *Courtesy of the Alan Santa Cruz Collection.*

Picayune published an article about the Baricevs' Auditorium Restaurant, listing frog legs, hard- and soft-shell crabs and shrimp as featured on the menu. The restaurant was located directly across the street from the municipal auditorium and was considered one of the most popular places in the city for those who demanded and enjoyed excellent cuisine. The article indicated that Joseph P. had been in the New Orleans restaurant business for twelve years. Known as Joe by thousand of his patrons, he was described as friendly, with an agreeable personality, while his ability as a chef gained him citywide respect.

The article stated that the Auditorium had always been known for short orders of sandwiches and seafood. All who had eaten there agreed that Joseph's shrimp, crawfish, boiled crabs or soft-shell crabs, frog legs and any other delicacies they tried allowed them to walk away well satisfied. The Auditorium was a twenty-four-hour business with a delivery service. The location near the municipal auditorium attracted patrons of carnival balls and other functions held there. The article ended with the fact that the restaurant was clean and had great service and reasonable prices. By 1935, Joseph P. and his brother Peter were working at Peter's Restaurant on 326 Baronne for William J. Peters.

After being involved in the restaurant business in New Orleans for over twenty-six years, Joseph P. Baricev; his wife, Jessie; and children, Joseph F., Robert and Victor, returned to Biloxi. In 1948, the family returned to the restaurant business. Baricev's Restaurant and Lounge opened its doors at 633 West Beach. In 1949, Joseph and Jessie's son Joseph F. was operating French Restaurant at 209 West Howard Avenue. His grandfather Petar was listed as the cashier. By 1952, Robert had joined his brother at the French Restaurant.

On November 18, 1951, tragedy struck the family when their beloved patriarch, Petar Baricev, passed away. By 1954, both businesses became a joint venture, with Joseph P., Jessie, Joseph F., Victor J. and Robert listed at Baricev's and the French Restaurant. On October 9, 1957, Tereza Buljacic Baricev died. Sometime between 1965 and 1967, the French Restaurant changed hands, and Greg Lawrence became the proprietor.

On September 9, 1965, Hurricane Betsy made landfall on Grand Isle, Louisiana, and continued a northern course. Along the Mississippi Gulf Coast, heavy rains, flooding and wind damage occurred. Baricev's Seafood Harbor was destroyed. In 1966, the *Times-Picayune* reported that Mr. and Mrs. Joseph P. Baricev had opened a new seafood restaurant in a steel and concrete building overlooking the gulf. Business was good for Baricev's Restaurant as well as the whole Mississippi Gulf Coast.

Baricev's Restaurant. *Courtesy of the Alan Santa Cruz Collection.*

Baricev's Restaurant interior. *Courtesy of the Alan Santa Cruz Collection.*

Then, on August 17, 1969, a hurricane named Camille devastated the Mississippi Gulf Coast and destroyed Baricev's Restaurant. In 1970 during the recovery, Mr. Sandoval and his staff with the United States Small Business Administration (SBA) visited the area around the Buena Vista Hotel. The SBA provided support to entrepreneurs and small businesses in the aftermath of Camille. Sandoval and his staff visited with Joseph P. Baricev and the workers rebuilding Baricev's Restaurant. As the group departed the building, one of the SBA men indicated that these folks never quit. After being rebuilt, Baricev's Restaurant continued to offer local seafood, Creole dishes, stuffed flounder, oysters Baricev and Creole gumbo. Additional items offered were steaks and southern fried chicken. Once again, Baricev's Restaurant was a favorite of locals and tourists alike. By the early 1990s, a new business of casinos became the topic of conversation and then a reality. In 1993, the Biloxi Belle Casino leased the Baricev's building and property. After forty-five years of service to the Gulf Coast, Baricev's Restaurant closed its door for the last time.

On October 9, 1996, Jessie Traina Baricev passed away and was laid to rest in the Biloxi Cemetery. Three years later, Joseph Baricev died on December 9, 1999, and was buried next to Jessie. One old postcard indicated that Baricev's Restaurant was the originator of stuffed flounder. Today, the Beau Rivage Casino and Resort occupies the former location Baricev's Restaurant.

20

Gus Stevens Restaurant and Supper Club

On one visit to Burger Burger Restaurant in Biloxi for coffee and fellowship with the morning Burger Burger gang, Lynn and Sandra Patterson began to pass around an old, well-worn souvenir menu. The souvenir menu was from Gus Stevens Seafood Restaurant and Buccaneer Lounge and had been borrowed from Jimmy Manning. One look at the food—and especially the prices—and we all wished we could order our meal at these late 1950s and early 1960s prices. Of course, when one looks at prices of the late 1950s and early 1960s, we must remember that income of that period does not compare to today's income. In 1959, the average income per year in the United States was $5,000. The average cost of a home was about $12,400, and a new car was about $2,200.

Gus Stevens Restaurant and Buccaneer Lounge opened its door in 1947 on the corner of Beach Boulevard and Pat Harrison Avenue (today's Veterans Boulevard). Gus and Irene Stevens were the owners. The name changed slightly over the years. In the late '50s and early '60s, it was listed as Gus Stevens Seafood Restaurant and Buccaneer Lounge. During the late '60s and '70s, it was listed as Gus Stevens Restaurant and Supper Club.

Reviewing the menu, one finds that Gus Stevens offered the souvenir menu to its patrons at no cost. The menu had various pictures of the restaurant, lounge and the Biloxi Lighthouse and a map with local points of interest and Gulf Coast cities. The menu advertised Gus Stevens as the doorway to hospitality, offering the finest foods and gay entertainment on America's Riviera.

A Gus Stevens Restaurant and Supper Club menu. *Author's collection.*

Gus Stevens indicated that the restaurant's specialty was home cooking of barbecue, seafood, steaks, spaghetti dinners and southern fried chicken. To advertise the freshness of his food, the menu indicated that the chickens and pigs were fresh and came from the family's farm near Lizana, Mississippi. The Stevenses' Rainbow Ranch was located between Gulfport and Poplarville on Highway 53. The menu also indicated that eggs were gathered fresh every morning from the farm. Of course, the menu also advertised fresh seafood from the boats.

Then, of course, there was the Buccaneer Supper Lounge. Here, tourist and locals would dine, dance and be entertained. Gus Stevens advertised nightly entertainment and floorshows, for a cover charge. The menu indicated that stars of the stage, TV, silver screen and radio would entertain patrons.

Gus Stevens Good Morning Club Breakfast was served from 7:00 a.m. to 11:00 a.m. For $0.85, you could have one egg; ham, bacon or the Stevenses' special pig sausage; toast with jelly; and coffee. The same breakfast with two eggs would have cost you $1.30. For the big eaters, you could get a hickory-smoked ham steak with two eggs, toast with jelly and coffee for $1.50.

The barbecue pit specials were barbecued ribs and barbecued chicken. For $2.45, you could enjoy barbecued ribs with coleslaw and French fries. Half of a barbecued chicken served with French fries cost $2.25.

The Western-style steaks varied from sirloin, prime rib, T-bone and filet mignon. Steak prices began at $4.50 or $5.50, but a large, double-sirloin steak for two cost $8.50. Another of Gus Stevens's specialties was spaghetti dishes. Spaghetti with Italian meat sauce cost $1.15; with meatballs, $1.95; and with meat sauce and a veal cutlet, $2.35.

Gus Stevens had a great seafood platter with trout tenderloin, fried shrimp, fried oysters, stuffed crab, coleslaw, French fries and tartar sauce for $2.50. Of course, there were also entrées of shrimp, oysters, flounder, snapper and stuffed lobster.

Gus Stevens Restaurant and Buccaneer Lounge advertisements in *Down South* magazine, July/August 1972. *Author's collection.*

The menu also invited patrons to visit the Buccaneer Lounge after dinner for a wonderful floorshow, fine music and dancing. One could enjoy cocktails like a martini or Manhattan for $0.50. A highball made from Canadian Club and Seagram VO would cost $0.75 while Seagram 7 Crown was $0.60. Mixed drinks like a Singapore Sling would cost $1.50 while a Tom Collins or whiskey sour cost $0.75. Beer was served in the bottle for $0.40 each.

Gus and Irene Stevens appear to have possessed a natural ability to not only offer good food and drink but also to entertain their guests. Their customers, in return, continued to patronize Gus Stevens Restaurant and Supper Club. The Stevenses were pioneers of the hospitality industry and operated a one-of-a-kind restaurant and nightclub. Some entertainers came from New Orleans.

Constantine Gus Stamatios Kouvarakis was born on May 30, 1911, in Chester, Pennsylvania, to Stamatios Steve and Catherine Coronis Kouvarakis of Greece. Desiring a warmer climate, the Kouvarakis family returned to Greece. In Greece, Stevens's brother, Theologos (or Ted), was born on the Island of Patmos. When Gus was about seventeen years old, the family returned to the United States, this time to the warm climate of the Mobile area. Here, Gus and his brother, Ted, changed their surname to Stevens. In Alabama, Ted and Gus operated their first restaurants, the Juicy Pig and the White Palace. During World War II, Gus enlisted in the navy reserve only to be released due to his poor eyesight.

Sometime between 1944 and 1945, he made a decision to open a restaurant in Houston, Texas, but fate would alter his course. While traveling to Houston, he stopped in Biloxi and took a room at the Buena Vista Hotel. He noticed a restaurant on the south side of Beach Boulevard and decided to eat there. The owner was Bob Thompson, and soon Gus was conversing and drinking with Bob. During the course of the conversation, Bob suggested Gus purchase his restaurant but indicated that Gus most likely did not have the money. Gus produced $1,000 in cash as a down payment, and Bob and Gus wrote a bill of sale on a paper napkin. He opened Gus Stevens Café and Bar at 625 West Beach Boulevard, the current location of Beau Rivage Casino.

In 1946, the winds of fate once again blew favorably for Gus. One day, several young women of Greek descent entered Gus's restaurant with a request for a donation for the Greek War Relief effort. One of the young women was Irene Mitchell, who was their spokesperson. Irene was the daughter of John Mitchell and Helen Abazzi Katradis. The original Mitchell family name was Katradis, but Irene's father, like Gus, had used his middle name as his surname. After looking into the deep blue eyes of Gus Stevens, Irene knew she had found her soul mate. A romance developed between the young couple, and on October 27, 1946, Gus Stevens and Irene Mitchell were married.

The future of the young couple looked good. Business was good, and during September 1947, the Stevenses had just stocked steaks and other meats for a big convention at the Buena Vista Hotel. Then on September 19, 1947, a large storm struck the Mississippi Gulf Coast. Gus and Irene waded into their business and removed two bags of money. Irene, with moneybags in hand, settled in at the post office while Gus assisted other Biloxians. Along the Biloxi beachfront, all wooden structures were flattened. Boats, pilings, piers, factories, buildings, automobiles, furniture and more were scattered along the shore. In Biloxi's business district, only two structures on the south side of Highway 90 survived—the yacht club and the USO building. The Stevenses' restaurant was destroyed.

Once again, Gus found himself starting over and purchasing another Bob Thompson restaurant. The drive-in restaurant was located on the corner of Beach Boulevard and Pat Harrison. Between 1947 and 1949, Gus Stevens operated the Gus Stevens Drive In Restaurant.

Gus Stevens Restaurant and Supper Club, Highway 90. *Courtesy of the Alan Santa Cruz Collection.*

The hectic day-to-day business of running a restaurant did not prevent Gus and Irene from starting a family. They had three children, Elaine, Kathryn and Steve. Somewhere around 1949, Gus and Irene decided to remodel their drive-in into a walk-in establishment under the name of Gus Stevens Restaurant and Lounge. When Gus and Irene added live entertainment, a new evolution on the Biloxi Strip had begun. Before long, Gus Stevens had become the entertainment hot spot of the Gulf Coast. Entertainers from the stage, screen and radio began to entertain patrons. Entertainers like Andy Griffith, Jerry Lee Lewis, Brother Dave Gardner, Mel Torme, Justin Wilson and Jayne Mansfield preformed at Gus Stevens. Some entertainers, like Johnny Rivers, came from New Orleans. By 1958, the restaurant was known as Gus Stevens Seafood Restaurant and Buccaneer Lounge.

In 1967, Jayne Mansfield was booked at Gus Stevens from June 23 to July 4. Jayne performed at 9:00 p.m. and 11:00 p.m., with an additional 1:00 a.m. performance on weekends. Jayne, Sam Brody (her attorney and lover) and her children—Miklos, Zoltan and Mariska Hargitay—flew into Keesler Air Force Base. Later plans were to tour the base, entertain troops and visit wounded soldiers back from Vietnam.

On June 29, Jayne was scheduled for an interview on an early morning talk show at WDSU-TV in New Orleans. Jayne had requested that Gus furnish a limousine and chauffeur to take her to this interview. Gus told her he had neither but agreed to loan her Irene's 1966 Buick Electra. Gus then asked employee Ronnie Harrison to drive them to New Orleans. The twenty-year-old college student reluctantly agreed. Sometime after her last show on June 28, Jayne, Sam, Jayne's three children and driver Ronnie Harrison began that fateful drive to New Orleans.

The car followed the winding Highway 90 from Mississippi to Louisiana. Around 2:25 a.m.,the Buick Electra rounded a foggy curve and slammed into an eighteen wheeler. The fog had been created by a City of New Orleans mosquito fogger truck. Upon impact, the car slid under the rear of the trailer. Jayne Mansfield, Sam Brody and Ronnie Harrison were killed instantly. Jayne's children, along with two of her dogs, survived.

For the Stevens family, the tragedy struck home in more ways than one. Unknown to Gus and Irene was the fact that their daughter Elaine and Ronnie Harrison had planned to elope. Elaine was carrying Ronnie's baby. Like so many young women in the '50s and '60s, when this was discovered, she was sent away to have her baby and give her up for adoption. Unlike the unknown that so many of these young women lived with, Elaine was reunited with her daughter, Angie Lathrop, in 2000.

Gus Stevens Restaurant and Buccaneer Lounge. *Courtesy of the Alan Santa Cruz Collection.*

Gus Stevens Restaurant and Supper Club continued to do business, but some of the luster was gone. In 1975, the doors of Gus Stevens closed for the last time. Tragedy once more visited the Stevens family on March 10, 1989, with the death of Gus Stevens. Gus Stevens Restaurant and Supper Club has faded into our memories and into the pages of history.

21

Friendship House Restaurant

Historically, both corners of DeBuys Road and Highway 90 were the locations of restaurants. Of course, the Friendship House is the one that most of us remember. The Friendship House was located on the east side of DeBuys Road and Highway 90, but interestingly enough, the history of the Friendship House is tied to another restaurant that was on the west side of DeBuys.

The Triple X Inn was owned by Homer Martin. In the 1931 Gulfport city directory, the Triple X was listed as being west of DeBuys Road. Homer was born on November 8, 1902, in Neshoba County. By 1928, he had moved to Mississippi City. In April of the same year, he met Ida Mae Ladnier at a party at the home of C.R. Switzer in Fernwood. On November 14, 1933, Homer Martin and Ida Ladnier were married. Homer and Ida's home was located east of DeBuys Road, near the Triple X Inn.

In 1937, the *Daily Herald* reported that the Triple X stand had changes hands. The Triple X stand on DeBuys was moved to the east side of DeBuys Road and Highway 90 and turned to face west. An addition to the Triple X stand was the construction of a dance floor. The stand was renamed Dinty Moore's Place and sold sandwiches and other refreshments. The new owner's name was not released to the public. Some oral history indicates that Homer Martin continued as the owner. In 1939, Edwin King Beasley is listed in the *Daily Herald* as trading as Dinty Moore and appears to have been the owner.

Edwin Beasley was born on March 21, 1907, in Lewisburg, Tennessee. He moved to Harrison County to work in real estate. In Mississippi City, he

The Friendship House and Beasley Seafood Restaurant. *Courtesy of the Maritime and Seafood Industry Museum.*

met June Glevis Grant. June was born on November 3, 1916, in Nevada, Missouri. Edwin and June were married on August 5, 1938, in Mississippi City. In 1940, the Grove Club Lounge built a new structure next to Dinty Moore's Restaurant. The DeBuys and Beach intersection was becoming a busy area. By the mid-1940s, Dinty Moore's became Beasley's Seafood Restaurant, and the owner was Edwin Beasley. In the 1949 Gulfport city directories, the restaurant was listed as Beasley's Restaurant and Tourist Court, located in Mississippi City.

On July 14, 1949, the restaurant once again changed hands. Edwin and June Beasley sold the restaurant to Jim and Mary Myers. Afterward, Edwin and June Beasley retired to Polk County, Florida. Edwin passed away on April 17, 1982, and June died on February 23, 1989.

Jim Myers was born on October 25, 1894, in Palmyra, Tennessee. During World War I, he served in the army's Eighty-first Motor Transport Division, fighting in France and Germany. Like many soldiers in World War I, he contracted the Spanish flu. To most, it was a death sentence, but not for Jim Myers. After the war, he went on to work in the wholesale produce industry in Nashville. It wasn't long before he heard the call of the Gulf Coast.

By 1931, Jim had entered the restaurant industry, working for Burros and Webber Cafeterias in Memphis. In 1933, he went to work for the Toddle

House chain. Chain restaurants were a new industry. In this new industry, Jim's job would take him to forty-two states, but one state, Mississippi, would catch his eye and, later, his heart.

In 1941, he became manager of the Kentucky's Blue Boar Cafeteria chain. It was here that he met Mary Anderson Parrish, who was the head hostess for the Blue Boar. Mary was born on October 19, 1918, in Papinville, Missouri. In 1933, her parents, Charles and Ada Montgomery Anderson, moved their family to Louisville. Mary married William Parrish around 1938, and they had one child, Peggy Anne, before the marriage ended. Mary's career at the Blue Boar was on the fast track, and she soon became head hostess. In early 1947, Jim could not resist the call of the Mississippi Gulf Coast. He moved to the coast, and Mary and her daughter came with him. They were married in Pascagoula on July 8, 1947. They were blessed with two more children, James in 1948 and Mary "Suzie" in 1949. Their journey was just beginning.

On the coast, Jim and Mary entered a partnership with Jack Fairchild. Their careers in the Gulf Coast restaurant industry began at Fairchild's Restaurant and Cottages in Mississippi City. On July 14, 1949, Jim and Mary purchased Beasley's Seafood Restaurant and renamed it the Friendship House Restaurant.

All those years of labor in the restaurant industry paid off for Jim and Mary. Improvements and three expansions began to reshape the

The Friendship Restaurant and the old Dinty Moore's. *Courtesy of the Alan Santa Cruz Collection.*

restaurant. After just six months, the Myerses knew they had made the right choice. Over time, improvements to the sand beach and Highway 90 brought more traffic and more business. The Meyerses started with 12 employees in 1949, and by 1955, they employed 106. The original restaurant and lounge could accommodate 50 guests, and by 1955, the remodeled restaurant could accommodate 425 guests. The number of employees reached 125 during the Friendship House's heydays.

Advertisements for the Friendship House stated that the restaurant was known from coast to coast as "Your Host on the Gulf Coast." The menu boasted fresh-from-the-Gulf shrimp, fish, crabs, scallops and broiled flounder in butter. Of course, seafood gumbo, fried chicken and tender steaks rounded out the Friendship House menu. Another menu item was Florida lobster. No one else along the Gulf Coast would use the smaller Florida lobster. Jim stuffed them with crabmeat, shrimp and other Gulf delicacies. The restaurant industry of his day credited him with changing the fate of the Florida lobster from trash to delicacy. After visiting the Friendship House, Arkansas columnist Mildred Woods wrote, "Napoleon said an army travels on its stomach—well, so does a tourist."

In 1954, the first commercial microwaves were produced. The Friendship House was the first to use the Radar-Range. The future of the Friendship House and the Myers family looked very promising indeed. *Deep South* magazine reported, "The Friendship House microwave could cook a sirloin in 26 seconds, a 3 pound chicken in 9 minutes, broil a 1½ pound lobster in 3 minutes, and a baked potato in 2 minutes."

The future of the Friendship House looked good with Jim and Mary Myers as the host and hostess. Due to Jim and Mary, the restaurant became known as the "Home of Southern Hospitality." In 1956, some of the Friendship House's fringe benefits were the restaurant's five-cent cup of coffee with unlimited refills. Hot biscuits and preserves were served free. They also advertised that "oleo" was not "tolerated [here], only sweet creamy butter." One could order anything you wanted from native to imported seafood. That same year, they acquired the nearby Grove Club lounge.

On September 20, 1956, a *Times-Picayune* article listed Mississippi eating places. Their picks were the Cabana Beach Motel, the Longfellow House and the Friendship House. The Myerses also opened a putt-putt (miniature golf) course. In 1958, the nationwide Putt-Putt Golf Course held a Miss Putt-Putt contest. Joan Honeycutt became the Friendship House course's Miss Putt-Putt 1958.

The Friendship House menu. *Author's collection.*

The early 1960s were full of political turmoil and personal pressures on the Myers family and their Friendship House and Cottages. On November 11, 1963, Jim and Mary Myers announced that the Friendship House had been sold to the Brennan Family of New Orleans. On November 12, the Brennans took over operations. They announced that the current "menu, prices and casual resort type dining" would carry on.

The Brennan family eventually added their own color to the Friendship House. One item that hung on the wall was an 1846 punt gun. Legend indicates that the swivel-mounted gun was mounted on the bow of a skiff and used in duck hunting. The gun was purchased in the estate sale of a deceased wealthy New Orleanian. The claim was that the gun could kill 150 ducks in one shot.

By the 1970s, the Friendship House boasted a Sunday jazz brunch from 11:00 a.m. to 3:00 p.m. Performers from the French Quarter jazzed up the Sunday brunch. Famous New Orleans chef Paul Prudhomme was executive chef over the Friendship House and five other Brennan restaurants. Prudhomme's duty was to create the dishes and teach the personnel in each restaurant how to cook them.

The success that the Myerses acheived while at the helm of the Friendship House began to fade. By 1981, the Brennan family closed the historic Friendship House, ending a thirty-two-year history.

Jim and Mary Myers had successfully operated the Friendship House from 1949 to 1963. Over the course of several years, the Myerses promoted the Eight Flags venture in Florida, traveled and became associated with a Holiday Inn in Venice, Florida. Eight Flags was known to most along the coast as the Eight Flags Deer Ranch and Six Gun Junction. In 1970, they returned to their home in Mississippi City and the Log House Restaurant and Lounge would open and begin its journey. In October, their new restaurant opened half a block north of their original Friendship House.

Mary once again became the hostess with the mostest by keeping customers happy and letting them experience her own variety of southern hospitality. As always, Jim oversaw the operations of the restaurant to ensure quality food and service. The Log House was a steel frame building with an exterior appearance of a log house or pioneer trading post. One new member to their staff was their twenty-three-year-old son, James Jr.

The Friendship House advertisements in *Down South*, September–October 1969. *Author's collection.*

In 1970, the restaurant day began at 6:00 a.m. with breakfast. By midday, one could enjoy the luncheon specials. Of course, in the evening, fine dining and drinks were served to the Log House guests. Once again, a Myers restaurant became the gathering place for tourists and locals.

After fourteen years of running the Log House, the Meyerses' daughter Susie Wilson and their son-in-law Jerry Wilson took over the day-to-day management for Jim and Mary. The daily breakfast was discontinued. The only exception was the Saturday and Sunday brunch, from 10:00 a.m. to 12:00 p.m. The Log House continued to be open for lunch and supper.

On October 14, 1984, the Myerses were honored at the Biloxi Hilton. They were presented with keys to the Gulf Coast by Waveland mayor Johnny Longo. A proclamation was presented from the City of Biloxi by Susan Hunt and the City of Gulfport by Dale Hetrick. A plaque was presented by the Harrison County Board of Supervisors. Another plaque was presented by the Gulf Coast Restaurant Association for the Meyerses' excellent service in the Gulf Coast restaurant trade since 1947. President Himbert Sinopoli stated that forty years ago, the

Myerses' vision was the reason we have seen food service on the coast revolutionized. Unfortunately, Jim had been hospitalized and was unable to attend this honorable celebration, but Mary accepted the awards on behalf of them both.

On November 5, 1985, Jim passed away and was laid to rest in the Long Beach Cemetery. In October 1988, Charlie Anderson, Mary's brother, began to manage the Log House for Mary, who had had a stroke. On August 24, 1989, the Log House closed its doors after lunch for the last time.

On October 19, 1998, her birthday and thirteen years after Jim's death, Mary passed away and was laid to rest near her husband. The Friendship House and Log House have faded into our history, but the legacy of Jim and Mary Myers continues in the memories of locals and tourists who were touched by the Myerses' southern hospitality.

22

Baldwin Wood Lighthouse

During the years before Hurricane Camille, there was once a very unusual structure on East Beach between Main and Bellman Streets. For the tourist who had never visited the Mississippi Gulf Coast, it was one of those once in a lifetime structures you wanted to visit. The Baldwin Wood Lighthouse was a private lighthouse that had weathered many hurricanes, until Camille in 1969. For coast residents, it was a part of their past that had stood as long as they could remember. Even though it was called the Baldwin Wood Lighthouse, it was not built by the Wood family but by the Howard family. In some ways, this is the story of the Howard family, the 1800s Louisiana lottery, the Wood family and the wooden lighthouse.

Let us begin with the Howard family and the Louisiana Lottery. Of course, the Howard name has ties to Howard Avenue and the old Howard Memorial Hospital. Also, Biloxi school buildings throughout the history of Biloxi public schools bear the Howard name. All were named in honor of Frank, Harry and Annie Howard, the children of Charles and Marie Palmira Howard. Charles and Marie had another child, William, but little is known about him. Charles Howard was of English descent and arrived in New Orleans from Maryland in the mid-1800s. His wife, Maria Palmira Boullemet, was a New Orleans native.

Charles Turner Howard was born in Baltimore, Maryland, on March 4, 1832, to Richard Howard Turner and Elizabeth Patton. Yes, it appears Charles reversed his last and middle name for some unknown reason. He graduated from a Baltimore college and began drifting south. He began his

1907 view of the Baldwin Wood Lighthouse. *Courtesy of the Alan Santa Cruz Collection.*

career as a lottery agent working for the Kentucky and Havana lotteries. Sometime around 1852, his work brought him to New Orleans. Here, he met Maria Palmira Boullemet, and they married around 1854. From the union, they had four children who would carry the Turner name as their middle name.

In 1861, the Howard family moved to Biloxi. We know that their boys Harry and Frank were born in New Orleans. William was born in September 1861, possibly in Biloxi. On September 20, 1864, Maria Palmira gave birth to a daughter, Annie, in Biloxi.

Around 1866, the lottery firm of C.H. Murray & Co. of Kentucky hired Charles Howard to apply for a charter in Louisiana. Gambling in some form was common throughout Louisiana's history. In 1810, the Louisiana legislature passed an act that allowed the Episcopal church to run a $10,000 lottery. Today, we might call it a raffle. Lotteries for schools, local improvements, various organizations and other causes were common in Louisiana. The first charter failed, but the *New York Times* reported that

Howard was still paid $50,000 for pursuing the venture. In 1868, the family returned to New Orleans but maintained a home in Biloxi.

In 1868, the Louisiana legislature passed legislation for the state lottery. On August 26, 1868, the Louisiana State Lottery Company was formed and given exclusive rights to run a state lottery. Many very prominent Louisiana citizens became stockholders.

Charles Howard; his wife, Maria Palmira; and their children Harry, Frank and Annie had homes in Biloxi and New Orleans. The Howard family property in Biloxi extended from Bellman Street to Main Street and from the beach to Biloxi Back Bay. The Victorian-style home had a carriage house and stables behind the home. The one unusual aspect was the Victorian-style lighthouse in front of the Howard home. Charles Howard enjoyed sailing and was the owner of numerous sailing sloops. One rumor was that Charles built the lighthouse for one of his children who had become ill. While it makes for a nice story, the lighthouse was built for his own personal use.

Charles Howard, being the principle engineer of the Louisiana State Lottery Company, was made president. One of the interesting aspects of the lottery was the use of two famous Confederate generals to supervise the drawings. The involvement of P.G.T. Beauregard and Jubal A. Early was supposed to reflex the fairness of the drawings. Of course, both were paid a nice yearly salary for their time.

The Howard family home about 1914. *Courtesy of the Alan Santa Cruz Collection.*

The Louisiana state lottery was a smooth operation from 1868 until 1890. It was at this time that the United States Congress made it illegal for lottery tickets to be mailed. Before the law went into effect, the state lottery received thirty thousand letters. In 1890, the mail was one of the quickest means of sending and delivering the lottery tickets. This mail law would have, in time, ended the lottery, but the lottery's days were numbered even without this law. In 1892, the United States Supreme Court upheld a law making the Louisiana state lottery illegal.

During the life of the lottery, Charles not only amassed a fortune but also acquired three homes and numerous other properties. These homes were located on East Beach in Biloxi; St. Charles Street in New Orleans; and Ingleside, Dobbs Ferry, in New York. He also became a powerful businessman and a behind-the-doors politician. He was reported to have interests in two of New Orleans's newspapers and a sugar plantation in Louisiana. His generosity toward churches, schools, charities and other institutions was well noted.

In May 1885, the Howard family was spending the summer at their estate in New York. During a carriage ride, Charles was thrown from the carriage and severely injured. He remained in severe pain for three days and died on May 31, 1885. His remains were returned to New Orleans, and he was buried in the Metairie Cemetery. He was survived by his wife and three children. Two of his pallbearers were General P.G.T. Beauregard and Albert Baldwin Wood. General Beauregard was a family friend. Albert Baldwin Wood eventually purchased the Howard family home in Biloxi. After Charles Howard's death, his three children were left a fortune. In 1902, Maria Palmira Howard passed away, leaving her children the rest of the Howard estate that included the Biloxi property.

In Biloxi, the Howard family had been very active in the Church of the Redeemer. In 1891, a new church was constructed. Charles's son Harry Turner Howard donated the land. This structure was destroyed in 1969 by Hurricane Camille; only the bell tower was left. Before his death, Charles had donated the church rectory to Reverend Robert Hinsdale. The Ring in the Oak was just above the rectory walkway. The Ring in the Oak Tree is a freak of nature that formed a ring in one large limb. Added to this is a local Indian legend, so the ring has attracted considerable interest from tourists and locals alike.

Harry and Frank Howard were generous supporters of many of Biloxi's improvements. Some of these were artesian wells, parks and the Biloxi public school system. In 1898, the family built and donated a building to

1947 hurricane damage to the Baldwin Wood Lighthouse. *Courtesy of the Alan Santa Cruz Collection.*

be used as a school on Main and Water Streets. Then in 1902, Harry had another school built and donated on Point Cadet. These two schools were called Howard One and Howard Two. Additional property was donated to the city for parks and schools, and Central High School on Howard Avenue was built there.

Harry Howard served as mayor of Biloxi for three terms—1889, 1896 and 1897. Harry returned to New Orleans in 1902. In 1919, the Biloxi

Hospital Association purchased Harry's home on the corner of Nixon Street and Beach Road. Annie and Frank continued as dual residents in Biloxi and New Orleans.

There is a rumor that the Howard family built the Church of the Redeemer in 1891 for Annie's marriage. She was to marry in 1893, so this is just a rumor. The sad truth is that she was to be married on November 7, 1893, to Carter Harrison, mayor of Chicago. On October 28, 1893, Mayor Harrison was shot at his Chicago residence. Annie Howard was in Chicago preparing for the pending wedding. She had returned to the Harrison house a few minutes after the assassination, but Mayor Harrison had already passed away. The following week, Carter Harrison and Annie Howard had planned a special train ride from Chicago to Biloxi for their marriage in the Church of the Redeemer. The *New Orleans Times* noted that Howard's grief was pitiable. Sadly, she returned to Biloxi alone.

Annie Howard found love again and married Walter Parrott. They were married on November 11, 1896, in St. James Church in London. She died on October 21, 1904, in London. On October 24, 1911, Frank Howard passed away in a New York hospital. On the date of his funeral, in New Orleans and Biloxi, schools were closed in his memory. A memorial was held at the Biloxi High School with prayer, song and a eulogy reflecting on the generosity Frank had bestowed on Biloxi. Harry, who had moved to New Orleans, died on February 19, 1930.

This was the end of the generosity of the Howard family in Biloxi. In 1912, Albert Baldwin Wood purchased the Howard family home and the lighthouse that would soon bear his name. Albert Baldwin Wood was born in New Orleans on December 1, 1879. His parents were John S. Wood of Pennsylvania and Octavia Bouligny of New Orleans. In New Orleans, he graduated from Tulane University in 1899 and received the Glendy Burke Award in mathematics. In 1899, the New Orleans sewerage and water board took over the drainage commission. The board hired twenty-year-old Baldwin Wood, as he was known. Baldwin was in charge of pump inspection and soon became fascinated with pumps. Using his degree in mathematics, he began to work on designs for a new pump.

On April 29, 1908, he married Nola Bradford Smith of New Orleans. They purchased a home at 1225 Milan Street. In 1907, Baldwin was promoted to mechanical engineer. That same year, Baldwin designed a new twelve-foot pump called a screw pump. Today, the screw pump is known as a propeller pump. This new design allowed for continuous automatic operation of the pumping system. Baldwin patented his design, and his

The Baldwin Wood Lighthouse before 1969. *Courtesy of the Lynn and Sandra Patterson Collection.*

pumps still keep New Orleans dry today. In 1916, Baldwin designed the Wood Trash Pump for the sewerage disposal system.

He became world renowned when Holland (today the Netherlands) employed him to design a pumping system to work with its dikes to hold back the North Sea. In addition to the Holland project, he assisted Chicago, Milwaukee, Baltimore, San Franciso, Canada, Egypt, China and Dutch East Indies with their drainage and pump installations. His Wood Trash Pump was also used in the Panama Canal. In 1928, he designed a fourteen-foot pump that could move 450,000 gallons of water a minute. In fact, Baldwin's pumps kept New Orleans dry during and just after Katrina. That is, until the levees failed. After Katrina, the pumps were cleaned up and put back in service. Some of Baldwin's pumps have been in service for over eighty years with little or no problems. His design is still used in new pumps installed in New Orleans.

Baldwin Wood purchased Frank Howard's Biloxi home about 1912. The Woods family members split their time between Milan Street in New Orleans and East Beach, Biloxi. In Biloxi, Baldwin Wood found his second love, the sloop *Nydia*. The vessel was built in 1897 at Johnson Shipyard in Biloxi. Its first owner was John A. Rawlins, a New Orleans native and Gulf Coast yachtsman. The vessel was named after one of the characters in *The Last Days of Pompeii*. Nydia was the blind slave girl who tried to save herself by jumping into the sea. Baldwin anchored the *Nydia* just south of the Wood family home. Every weekend, he returned to Biloxi to sail his beloved *Nydia*. The *Nydia* was stolen on one occasion but recovered. After that incident, the Baldwin Wood lighthouse was set to keep the *Nydia* lit from dusk to dawn.

Baldwin Wood was the general superintendent of the Sewerage and Water Board of New Orleans. His weekends and off time were spent in Biloxi, usually sailing the *Nydia*. By 1947, the Wood family had been living in Biloxi for about thirty-five years. On September 19, 1947, a category four storm hit the Mississippi Gulf Coast. Damages from the 1947 storm were over $110 million in 1947 dollars.

On the Woods' property, the lower floors of the wooden lighthouse were gutted and the lighthouse toppled. Using a pulley system, Baldwin Wood had the lighthouse righted and elevated, while the first floor was repaired. He restored it to its original state using the same materials and building methods that were originally used.

On May 10, 1956, Baldwin Wood left his office in New Orleans for Biloxi and an afternoon sail. He had two of his employee helping with his vessel. The two young men were Amos Tillman and George Quave. As usual, Wood sailed alone that afternoon. He sailed the *Nydia* from his wharf in front of his home down the channel. He suddenly slumped at the tiller, but the vessel continued to sail. Tillman and Quave noticed the vessel sailing errantly, and they could no longer see Wood. Captain Louis Gorenflo, aboard his vessel the *Sailfish*, noticed that Wood was slumped over and immediately pursued him. Captain Gorenflo was able to get close enough for his deckhand Joe

House of Treasures, the former Howard and Woods families home, 1960s. *Courtesy of the Lynn and Sandra Patterson Collection.*

Nicovich to board the *Nydia*. At this point, the *Nydia* was ten feet from some pilings, but Nicovich corrected its course and sailed it to Wood's wharf. Biloxi police and an ambulance were summoned. Detective Dominic Fallo and Officer Veen Lee were sent to investigate while Wood was rushed to the hospital. He was pronounced dead upon his arrival, and his body was transferred to Bradford Funeral Home. He was returned to New Orleans and buried in the Metairie Cemetery.

About 1963, the City of Biloxi acquired the Wood property. It intended to use the area to promote cultural activities and as a tourist attraction. On September 10, 1964, the *Daily Herald* announced the formal opening of the home as the House of Treasure. The *Daily Herald* reported the Victorian home still had its valuable collections "of silver, china, porcelain, tapestries, carpets, period furniture and objects d'art."

In addition to this, a collection of George Ohr pottery and his portrait were on display on the second floor of the home. The article noted that there was a sign near the Baldwin Wood Lighthouse advertising the House of Treasure. It also indicated that the lighthouse had been recently restored with natural finished cedar siding and white trim.

On August 17, 1969, Hurricane Camille struck the Mississippi Gulf Coast. The Baldwin Wood Lighthouse, which had weathered numerous storms, was destroyed. The House of Treasure, though still standing, was beyond repair. Wood's beloved sloop *Nydia* is now one of the main exhibits in the Maritime and Seafood Industry Museum.

23

Biloxi's USO and Community Center

In August 1966, I remember someone telling me that the Biloxi Community Center was on fire. A few days later, I saw the charred remains of the once bustling social center. I remember my first visit to the building as a child and how enormous I thought the building was. When I got older, I joined the Boy Scouts and attended Boy Scout functions in the center. As teens, my brother, John, and I would go to teen dances at the center. I have fond memories of dancing to bands from Mobile and New Orleans, especially New Orleans's own Irma Thomas.

Yes, the Biloxi Community Center was full of memories of my generation but also held the memories of the Greatest Generation. Built as a USO center, it opened its doors on March 14, 1942. Of 260 USO centers built in the United States, it was one of the largest. Its sponsor was the National Catholic Community Services (NCCS), a member of the USO. The NCCS's purpose was to serve the spiritual, social, educational and recreational needs of GIs and civilian defense workers and, of course, their families.

In early January 1942, the decision was made to build a USO in Biloxi. During construction, a temporary USO center was set up in Biloxi's armory on the corner of Railroad Street and Fayard Street. Carl Fischer had been appointed Biloxi USO director. The temporary center offered a snack bar and lounge with reading materials and radios. GIs could visit the information desk and comfort station, play games and attend dances. John T. Collins, a local architect, remodeled the armory. Mayor Louis Braun furnished oyster shells to fill the area in front of the armory.

Every Wednesday night, there was a dance with music by Russell Sessions and his post–air force dance band. Every Monday night, there were free dance classes for GIs. The game room offered shuffleboard, ping pong, checkers and card games. There was a desk and materials for writing letters home. From January 26 to March 4, 1942, fifty thousand sheets of paper were used by GIs to write letters.

On Saturday, March 14, the new Biloxi USO center opened on the southeast corner of Beach Boulevard and Main Street. Attending the gala opening were local leaders, military leaders and members of the Jewish Welfare Board and the NCCS. Invitations were sent to the general public, officers at Keesler Field and officers at the Biloxi Coast Guard station. Also, invitations were sent to young ladies in Biloxi and surrounding communities. About 2,500 attended the ceremonies, and an additional 1,000 or more toured the Biloxi USO building. Music for the evening began with a concert by the Biloxi High School band, under the direction of Professor M.M. Flowers. During intermission, local and enlisted talent entertained the crowd.

The opening ceremonies' color guard was made up of army and navy personnel and veterans. Warren Jackson, Biloxi Chamber of Commerce secretary, was master of ceremonies. Reverend C.H. Gunn and Father

Biloxi USO club on Highway 90, 1942. *Courtesy of the Alan Santa Cruz Collection.*

William Leech gave the invocation. "God Bless America" was led by Private Robert Blair of Steubenville, Ohio. Military personnel and civilian leaders presented eleven short speeches. Some of the local speakers were Ralph E. Dawley, a member of Biloxi's defense recreational committee; Dr. R.W. Burnett, a member of the Biloxi Chamber of Commerce; May Louis Braun; and Dewey Lawrence, county supervisor. During a grand march of USO personnel, a long line of young women in their pretty dance frocks paraded across the floor.

The program ended in a dance with the fourteen-piece Keesler Air Force Base dance orchestra, under the direction of Corporal Russell Sessions. Robert McManus of Biloxi was one of the members of this band. During the session, the band was joined by additional singers and dancers—Billy Frith, Robert Klinger, Howard Crawford, Paul Rafferty, Joyce Davis, Bernard Meyer, Harry James, Peter Banzerino, Norman Messinger, Louise Frith and Emile Christopher.

The Biloxi USO was built on land belonging to the City of Biloxi. The building was constructed at a cost of $110,000 in 1942 dollars. Of the overall cost, $90,000 was a grant from the Public Works Defense Administration. The rest of the money came from contributions from Harrison County and inner harbor and recreational funds.

The building was 155 by 110 feet. On the east and west sides were wings that were 10 by 40 feet. The main dance hall was 103 by 110 feet. At that time, it was most likely the largest dance floor in Mississippi. Of course, the large dance floor was built to be a multipurpose gymnasium and auditorium. There was ample seating for more than two thousand individuals. It also served as a gym for basketball, volleyball, boxing, badminton, table tennis and many other sports. There was a locker room with showers where the center furnished towels, soap and shaving gear free of charge.

The purpose of the Biloxi USO was to provide moral support, recreational services and a home away from home for servicemen. One could get a free cup of coffee, watch a movie or listen to music on a radio. Games like bingo, cards and checkers were also offered. GIs could attend canteen dances, various social events and, of course, USO shows. A large lounge room with a snack bar and jukebox overlooked the Mississippi Sound. On Sunday afternoons, the lounge featured a buffet lunch followed by a session on classical music and musical discussions. There was also an outdoor porch. The Biloxi USO center, like others throughout the United States, recruited female volunteers to serve doughnuts, dance, attend social

A soldier from Kessler Field in front of the USO club, 1940s. *Courtesy of the Lynn and Sandra Patterson Collection.*

events and just talk with the troops. The facility also had a completely equipped dark room for photographers.

The large facility held dances on Wednesday and Saturday nights. The orchestras of Corporal Russell Sessions and Private Richard DeFilippo of Keesler Field furnished the music. Mrs. J.H. Beeman was in charge of the local entertainment committees.

In addition to taking care of GIs' physical, spiritual and social needs, the Biloxi USO handled personal needs. If a GI had legal problems, an illness in the family or other issues of a confidential nature, the USO would help.

The building was a USO until 1947. The USO was dissolved at that time, and the Catholic bishops' committee took over operations of the building. In 1949, the USO was reactivated and once again took over operations. In the early 1960s, the USO operations did not require the large facility.

In October 1961, the City of Biloxi and the USO swapped buildings. The Biloxi Community Center on Beach Boulevard became the USO, and the old USO building became the Biloxi Community Center. The city utilized the building for various events like Mardi Gras and the Biloxi Doll and Toy Fund. Organizations like the Pony League, the Colt

The right side the Biloxi Community Center, the former USO club, before October 1966. *Courtesy of the Maritime and Seafood Industry Museum.*

League, Pewee Football, Boy and Girl Scouts, local churches and other organizations used the building to host events. The city also hosted teen dances and recreational events.

On August 19, 1966, the Biloxi Fire Department responded to a fire at the Biloxi Community Center on Beach Boulevard. The fire was large enough that units from the cities of Pascagoula, Ocean Springs, D'Iberville, Gulfport and Keesler Air Force Base responded. The flames leaped fifty feet into the air, and soon the roof collapsed. In roughly ninety minutes, the fire had practically burned the entire building. Today, Biloxi's Veterans' Memorial, Purple Heart Memorial and surrounding park appropriately occupy the property where once a bustling social center stood.

24

Biloxi's City Hall and Market

Not too many people remember when Biloxi's City Hall was located on Main Street just north of Howard Avenue. In 1965, it was torn down in the name of progress. The sixty-eight-year-old building was, like a lot of things, just a victim of time.

In March 1894, a group of Biloxi citizens proposed a plan for a new court building. The building was to include the fire hall, city hall and a courtroom. During meetings and planning sessions, it was determined that the firemen wanted a separate fire hall. The new city hall was also to house the meat and vegetable market. The mayor and board of aldermen adopted an ordinance calling for a bond.

J.F. Barnes, a Greenville, Mississippi architect, was hired to draw up the plans for the three-story brick structure. The plans called for a building 50 by 180 feet. The structure would be located north of Pass Christian Road, present day Howard Avenue, in the middle of Main Street.

The strip of land running from the beach to the Back Bay had been donated to the city by Gaspar Didlier. While the strip south of Howard Avenue was only forty feet wide, the strip north of Howard Avenue was much wider, and the structure could be built there. The donation was made to build and operate a meat and vegetable market house. Didlier was to receive the profits from the market house for ten years, at which time the property would be deeded to the city. The market was built sometime before the 1860s and rebuilt in 1868 after a storm destroyed it.

Bids on the new building were taken, and on June 5, 1894, the mayor and aldermen awarded the bid to G.C. Taylor and Company of Meridian.

A front view of Biloxi's City Hall and Market, circa 1895. *Courtesy of the Alan Santa Cruz Collection.*

Taylor and Company bid $13,987.25 while John R. Harkness and John Eistetter, local builders, bid $14,690.

Before work could begin, a problem with the city charter had to be amended so the city would have the power to issue bonds in the amount of $15,000. To complicate matters, the Bank of Biloxi withdrew its offer to buy the bonds. At this point, Taylor and Company offered to buy the bonds but wanted to increase the construction cost to $15,000. The city council agreed, and in January 1895, the work began.

Even in what was considered the good old days, another problem arose when Taylor and Company skipped town without completing the contract. Unfortunately, just before skipping town, they had also convinced the council to advance them $3,000.

The council found itself with an uncompleted structure and no contractor. The newly formed Biloxi building company of John R. and G.A. Harkness agreed to finish the project for $4,240. The original bid was $13,987.25, but in the end, the cost was $16,117. The Harkness brothers completed the work by April 1896. On April 21, 1896, the building was dedicated. After the dedication, A. Simon was paid $348 to construct the stalls, shelves and counters for the new marketplace. The first council meeting at the new hall was held on May 7, 1896.

By the early 1920s, the city needed more room. So in 1922, C.E. Matthes, a local architect, drew up plans for an addition. On August 7, 1922, the council approved the addition. Just a few months earlier, the city had paid its final bond payment on the original building. W.H. Hunt, commissioner of public works, supervised the day-to-day work. The original building had inside stairs, but the addition added external stairs to the second floor on the south side. Two additions were added to the north side, and the open-air market stalls were enclosed. Then in the 1940s, another addition was added on the north side for the Keesler Air Force Base military police unit.

During its sixty-eight years of existence, the structure housed many aspects of the city and federal governments. These included city offices, city and federal courtrooms, the police department, the city jail, the waterworks department, the tax collector's office and the justice of the peace offices and courts. Other agencies were the state offices of the highway patrol drivers' licenses, the collector of the port for the District of Pearl River offices, the

A side view of Biloxi's City Hall and Market, circa 1900. *Courtesy of the Alan Santa Cruz Collection.*

Biloxi's City Hall and Market.
Courtesy of the Alan Santa Cruz Collection.

A 1940s picture of the Federal Building that in 1965 would become Biloxi City Hall.
Courtesy of the Alan Santa Cruz Collection.

social security office, the civil defense office, the American Red Cross, the veteran service center and the Harrison County Health Department. At one time, there was also a barbershop under its roof.

In 1965, the plan was to move city hall into the remodeled Federal Building (today's city hall) on Lameuse Street. The new jail and courtroom building had been constructed on McElroy Street (the present-day juvenile facility). The new brick jail's capacity was listed as 65 inmates and would have a padded cell and an isolation cell. The courtroom was built to seat 106 people.

The 1896 Biloxi city hall was once considered the most imposing and substantial city hall in the state. It had served the citizens of Biloxi as the seat of local government and hosted many events. In 1965, it became a sacrifice to the wrecking ball. The sixty-eight-year-old landmark became a victim of time and progress. It was replaced with a large median with flower beds and a large *B* that outlined where the old city hall once stood. In time, it, too, would fall victim to time and progress.

25

Pizzati Pavilion and the L&N Park

On March 17, 1915, the *Daily Herald* announced that plans were in the works for a dance pavilion in L&N Park. The open-air structure was to be constructed on the southwest corner of Fayard Street near the Louisville and Nashville Railroad station. This pavilion was made possible by Colonel Salvadore Pizzati. Due to his generosity, the pavilion would be named Pizzati Pavilion. Over time, the structure became part of Nativity BVM Parish's land. It served as a kindergarten room and also a band hall. Let us begin our journey by taking a look at Salvadore Pizatti, Biloxi's L&N Park and Pizzati Pavilion.

Salvadore Pizzati was born in Palermo, Italy, on September 2, 1839, to Italian army captain Michael Anthony and Mariana Pizzati. He enlisted as an ordinary seaman and served in this capacity for three years and spent another year as a merchant marine. In 1868, he moved to New Orleans. In New Orleans, he was given command of a few oceangoing schooners. During this time, he became friends with Captain Salvatore Oteri, who owned the Blackball Line of schooners. Under Oteri's employment, he flourished. While visiting the home of Oteri, he was introduced to Oteri's sister-in-law Francesco "Frances" Valenzano. The couple courted, and on May 22, 1872, they were married in New Orleans.

It wasn't long before Salvadore was a partner in S. Oteri & Company. Like so many New Orleanians before them, Salvadore and Frances Pizzati made many visits to and owned a home in Biloxi. Salvadore and Frances purchased property in Biloxi at 1832 West Beach Boulevard.

The Biloxi sign and arches marking the entrance to the L&N Park. *Courtesy of the Maritime and Seafood Industry Museum.*

In 1901, the Biloxi train depot was being replaced by a new depot. In addition to the new depot, the railroad company wanted to beautify the vacant lot and turn it into a park. The park would give visitors a chance to relax and stroll about while waiting for passenger trains. It was only natural that the depot and park would attract hotel business. The Kennedy Hotel and Hotel Chiapella were built on the edge of the L&N Park. At edge of the park was a sign on stone pillars bearing the word "Biloxi." The stone pillars were moved to the corner of Main Street and Highway 90, and a new Biloxi sign was mounted on them.

In March 1915, the philanthropy of the Pizzati family was felt in Biloxi. The *Daily Herald* reported that Colonel Pizzati wanted to donate money for the construction of a dance pavilion at Biloxi's L&N Park. The building contract was given to Collins Brothers Company. On June 18, 1915, the dance pavilion was dedicated as the Pizzati Pavilion. Alonzo Woodville of New Orleans; Professor Linfield, superintendent of the Biloxi public schools; and I. Heidenheim, representing the City of Biloxi, all delivered speeches during the dedication. All the speakers praised Pizzati for his philanthropy, his business sense and his other attributes. A danced followed the dedication ceremony, with music by the Herald Brass Band.

The Pizzati Pavilion near the train station, late 1920s. *Courtesy of the Lynn and Sandra Patterson Collection.*

By October 1915, the city mayor and aldermen, with the approval of Colonel Pizzati, took bids to enclose Pizzati Pavilion. This was due to the coming winter tourist season. It also became the meeting place for the Biloxi Tourist Club; club membership consisted of annual tourists who spent most of the winter season in Biloxi.

On December 30, 1915, Pizzati passed away in New Orleans at the age of seventy-six. Salvadore Pizzati mourned in both New Orleans and Biloxi. After his death, Frances lived in Biloxi until her death on October 3, 1919. The age of the automobile marked a decline in tourists arriving by train. Biloxi's L&N station and park were no exception. With the decline in rail travel, the nearby hotels were replaced by new developments. The park and pavilion lay vacant. Sometime between 1925 and 1948, the Pizzati family heirs donated the Pizzati Pavilion building to Nativity BVM. The building was used as a kindergarten during the 1940s and '50s; the Sacred Heart Girl School also used it as a band hall.

The L&N Railroad Company sold the park and pavilion properties to Nativity BVM Church on May 31, 1966. That same year, bids went out for the removal of the pavilion and construction of additional classrooms for Sacred Heart School and a parish youth hall. The demolition of the pavilion was completed on June 25, 1966. In the pavilion's northeast corner pier was

The L&N Park and the Pizzati Pavilion. *Courtesy of the Becky Rose Collection.*

a marble stone. Behind the stone was a bottle with a note written by William Collins Sr. in 1915. It contained a list of individuals who had constructed the pavilion. The list read: Henry Eisletter, brick mason; William Caillavet, Peter Cazeaux, John Collins Sr., John Collins Jr., W.J. Collins Sr. and George Collins Sr., carpenters; Philip Dellenger Sr. and Philip Dellenger Jr., painters; and Charles Brown, laborer. The marble slab bore the names of the donors, contractors and architect. Time has witnessed the demise of the L&N depot and park and the Pizzati Pavilion.

26

Point Cadet Plaza and the Maritime and Seafood Industry Museum

On August 29, 2005, Hurricane Katrina's waves pounded the Mississippi Gulf Coast. Around the mouth of the Bay of Biloxi, homes, businesses, cars, boats and anything else in the storm's path were torn to pieces or completely annihilated. On the western shore, the walls of the Maritime and Seafood Industry Museum began to collapse. The old hangar, known as Point Cadet Plaza, and its huge doors began to fall. Katrina was slowly beginning to destroy structures that had weathered numerous hurricanes and witnessed all kinds of events. All along the Mississippi Gulf Coast, the story was the same.

The first time man viewed the Bay of Biloxi, its beauty must have been very picturesque. Before Katrina, one needed only to cross the bridge from Ocean Springs or Biloxi to see the beauty of the Bay of Biloxi. In recent years, Biloxi's skyline had been altered by casinos and hotels. Now, thanks to Katrina, it has been altered for no good reason other than the whims of Nature. Before Katrina, there were two structures that had been a portion of the skyline since 1934. They were Point Cadet Plaza and the Maritime and Seafood Industry Museum. These two structures were once the home of a United States Coast Guard Air Station, which was commissioned on the east end of Biloxi on December 5, 1934. The air station operated from this location until March 1947.

On September 21, 1933, United States senator Pat Harrison of Mississippi issued a statement that President Roosevelt had approved the seaplane base at Biloxi. The Biloxi base would be one of three bases approved for gulf cities.

The United States Coast Guard Air Station administration and living quarters. *Courtesy of the Alan Santa Cruz Collection.*

The other cities were St. Petersburg, Florida, and Galveston, Texas. The Biloxi base would have a radio station, a machine shop, an administration building (that became the Maritime and Seafood Industry Museum) and a hangar. The hangar (Point Cadet Plaza) would be a one-hundred-square-foot structure that could accommodate five amphibious, twin-engine seaplanes. Additional construction would include runways, ramps and the dredging of a channel for the seaplanes.

When the base opened, there were thirty men, four officers and six planes assigned to it. The men would each work thirty hours a week. The first base commander was Lieutenant W.S. Anderson from Gloucester, Massachusetts. The duties of the Biloxi Coast Guard Air Station were aerial surveillance, searching for lost or disabled vessels, reporting navigation obstructions such as wrecks, handling medical or evacuation missions and law enforcement. Due to the large fishing fleet on the Gulf Coast, the Biloxi air station also dropped storm warnings to the fishermen. The planes had to fly low and slow to accurately drop the warning message. The warning message was placed in a floating wooden block that was painted yellow with a long, yellow cloth attached. For the pilot and crew of these amphibians, this was dangerous work. The Biloxi crews had many close calls and some damaged aircraft; however, through it all, they only lost one aircraft.

U. S.
COAST GUARD

QUICKSILVER
Biloxi Charter Boats

Above: The Maritime and Seafood Industry Museum after Hurricane Katrina. *Author's collection.*

Opposite, top: The Coast Guard air station in Biloxi, general muster in front of the seaplane hangar, 1946. *Courtesy of the Maritime and Seafood Industry Museum.*

Opposite, bottom: The exhibit of a one-hundred-year-old boat in the Maritime and Seafood Industry Museum before Hurricane Katrina. *Courtesy of the Maritime and Seafood Industry Museum.*

In December 1941, the United States entered World War II. From 1934 to World War II, the Biloxi air station had three to five aircraft and about 10 officers and 35 enlisted men. By the end of the war, 350 personnel would be attached to the Biloxi air station. The air station had begun antisubmarine patrols. During the early years of war, the seaplanes' armament and depth charges were jury rigged until systems were developed for these aircraft. The Biloxi air station was very successful in search-and-rescue operations of torpedoed merchant vessels and tankers.

On August 1, 1942, Pilot H. White and Radioman George H. Boggs, in their Grumman amphibian, attacked German U-boat *U-166* and sank it in the Gulf of Mexico. The year 1945 brought about the end of World War II and a reduction of personnel at the Biloxi air station. By the middle of 1946, there were eighteen aircraft, a crash boat, a fireboat, twelve officers and fifty enlisted personnel. In March 1947, the station was placed in caretaker status. Then, a 1947 storm did severe damage to the station's facilities. The Coast Guard then decided to turn the land, hangar, ramps, administration building, barracks and mess hall over to the City of Biloxi.

The Mississippi Army National Guard used the base for several years. In the early 1960s, the Biloxi–Ocean Springs Bridge and Highway 90 divided the property in half. The City of Biloxi converted the hangar, administration building and property north of Highway 90 into the International Plaza, which later became the Point Cadet Plaza. The plaza was then used for special events, festivals, farmers' markets and fishing rodeos. Many of us attended the Fais Do-Do, oyster festivals, fishing rodeos and the Seafood Festival. Before Katrina, the J.L. Scott Marine Education Center, Gorenflo's Marina Point, the fishing piers and a portion of the Point Cadet Marina had occupied the south section of the old air base.

In 1985, the historic administration building was transformed into the Maritime and Seafood Industry Museum. Some of the museum exhibits were "Working Boats," "Schooners and Luggers Sailing the Mississippi Sound," "A Pulling Skiff," "A Sailing Skiff," "Marine Blacksmith," a boatbuilding

The newly opened Maritime and Seafood Industry Museum, 2014. *Author's collection.*

exhibit, a collection of outboard engines, "Reed Guice Hurricane," "Light Cruiser USS *Biloxi*," French colonial exhibits and a timeline depicting the maritime history of the Mississippi Sound. Dr. Val Husley, a local Biloxian and former curator of the museum, had built a museum that the whole Mississippi Gulf Coast was proud of. Then, Katrina struck its deathblow. The portions of the museum and Point Cadet Plaza that it did not destroy were so damaged that they had to be removed with heavy equipment. The Maritime and Seafood Industry Museum struggled to find a new location and raise funds for a new museum. The museum was dedicated to the people who built the Mississippi Gulf Coast—the people who, after every hurricane, have rebuilt the city in any way necessary. This is the same inner strength that helped rebuild the Maritime and Seafood Industry Museum. In the end, it was decided to rebuild on the same location. The doors of the new museum opened on August 1, 2014, to much fanfare.

27

Eight Flags

On May 1, 1971, the *Daily Herald* reported that J&L Enterprises had donated a display of eight flags at the foot of DeBuys Road. The concrete sign, with its eight flags, became a landmark for local residents. If one was headed east, it read, "Welcome to Biloxi and Eight Flags"; headed west, it read, "Welcome to Gulfport and Eight Flags." The display was the brainchild of Don Jacobs. The eight flags referred to four tourist amusements owned by Jacobs, CEO of J&L Enterprises. These amusements were the Biloxi Shrimp Tour Train, Eight Flags Deer Ranch, Six Gun Junction and the Marine Life Oceanarium.

Donald "Don" Patrick Jacobs was born on May 10, 1926, in Des Moines, Iowa, to Harry and Mary Jacobs. On June 6, 1944, the eighteen-year-old joined the navy. During World War II, he served in the Pacific on board the USS *Harris* APA 2, a troopship. On June 4, 1946, he was honorably discharged from active duty. After his discharge, he attended and graduated from Marquette University in Milwaukee, Wisconsin. In 1949, while living in Milwaukee, he applied for World War II service compensation from the State of Iowa.

Around 1959, Don moved to the Mississippi Gulf Coast. In 1960, he is listed as the resident manager of Brown Friedman & Company Wholesale Shoes in Gulfport. All of this changed in 1961 as Don began his journey into the tourism industry. The *Times-Picayune* in New Orleans reported that, for the first time available to Mississippi Gulf Coast visitors, there was was a Biloxi Shrimp Tour Train located by the famous Biloxi Lighthouse.

An advertisement for the Biloxi Shrimp Tour Train, Eight Flags Deer Ranch and Six Gun Junction in *Down South*, May–June 1970. *Author's collection.*

The guided, fifty-minute, ten-mile tour took visitors to the shrimp and oyster fleet docks, canning factories on Back Bay and Point Cadet, Keesler Air Force Base, Old Biloxi Cemetery, historic and antebellum homes, glamorous hotels, Ring in the Oak and much more. Don billed his Biloxi Shrimp Tour Train as an unforgettable fun ride that was educational for children. He was just getting started.

On May 5, 1963, the *Times-Picayune* newspaper reported the Eight Flags Deer Ranch on DeBuys Road was a new attraction on the Gulf Coast. Don was a tourism visionary who realized the there were not many family-oriented amusements along the Gulf Coast. His new Eight Flags Deer

The Eight Flags Deer Ranch in the early 1960s. *Courtesy of the Alan Santa Cruz Collection.*

Ranch would be recorded in newsprint alongside other coast attractions. These main attractions were the Marine Life Oceanarium, excursion boats to Ship Island, Beauvoir and Old Spanish Fort in Pascagoula and, of course, his Biloxi Shrimp Tour Train. The deer ranch advertised that visitors would be amazed and thrilled as they hand fed, petted and photographed tame deer. In the deer ranch nursery, children could bottle-feed baby animals. In time, a bird vaudeville theatre was erected. In the arena were colorful macaws, drum-beating ducks and many more barnyard friends.

Don's broad imagination wasn't finished, as he also wanted to change a small part of South Mississippi into a Wild West town. The new amusement, Six Gun Junction, opened in 1964. It was located adjacent to the Eight Flags Deer Ranch on DeBuys Road, and for one admission price, you could visit both attractions. During the same period, large, themed or amusement parks—like Disneyland, Knott's Berry Farm and Six Flags over Texas—were operating. Locally, however, the nearest amusement park was Pontchartrain Beach in New Orleans.

Don's Six Gun Junction was billed as an authentic old frontier town. It was like stepping back in time to a bygone era. The ads referred to it as a point in time that was the most glamorous and adventure-packed days of American history. Part of the action was a shoot-out between the sheriff and

The Eight Flags sign between Biloxi and Gulfport, Mississippi. *Courtesy of the Lynn and Sandra Patterson Collection.*

Cancan girls and other cast members in the Red Dog Saloon. *Courtesy of the Alan Santa Cruz Collection.*

the bad guys as the town citizens and tourists looked on. One of the main attractions of Six Gun Junction was the Red Dog Saloon. The saloon was a fully functional lounge with entertainment. Of course, with a saloon there must be cancan girls, and there were. One ad read: "Wet your whistle as the Dolly Sisters entertain you with a whiz-bang live show right out of the Old West Saloons."

During the day, soft drinks were served, but in the evening hours, it was grownup fare. No Wild West show could be complete without a villain, a hero and a heroine in a miniature epic play. This melodramatic presentation was performed nightly with such titles as *He Ain't Done Right by Nell* and *Curse You, Jack Dalton*. The audience was encouraged to cheer the hero while hissing, booing and throwing peanuts at the villain. There were also Punch-and-Judy puppet shows.

Don first used the expression "Eight Flags" in 1971. He and J&L Enterprises become owners of the Marine Life Oceanarium in Gulfport. Don and J&L Enterprises donated a new landmark between Biloxi and Gulfport. The display of the eight flags that have flown over the Mississippi Gulf Coast was erected on eight thirty-five-foot poles and a concrete base. By 1972, Don's advertisements read, "Welcome to Eight Flags," a complex of resort attractions that included Six Gun Junction, the Eight Flags Deer Ranch, the Marine Life Oceanarium and the Biloxi Shrimp Tour Train.

A Wild West shootout in Six Gun Junction. *Courtesy of the Alan Santa Cruz Collection.*

Over time, he opened similar venues with similar themes. They included Floridaland in Sarasota, Deer Ranch in Panama City, Porpoise Island at Pigeon Forge, the *Harbor Queen* boat tour in Gulfport, as well as Florida and Marine Animal Productions.

By the 1980s, times were changing, and business was not as strong. In 1985, Don sold the Eight Flags complex at DeBuys Road to the Gulf Coast Community Hospital. Then the State of Mississippi made a decision to locate the state-owned J.L. Scott Marine Education Center in Biloxi. Don felt the marine education center, with its large aquariums full of sea life, placed theMarine Life Oceanarium in jeopardy. In 2005, Hurricane Katrina destroyed the Marine Life Oceanarium. On November 8, 2011, Donald "Don" Jacobs passed away in Gulfport. Many had dubbed him the father of the modern Gulf Coast tourism industry.

Bibliography

Books

City of Biloxi. *The Buildings of Biloxi: An Architectural Survey*. Biloxi, MS: 1976. Reprint 2000.

Dyer, Charles Lawrence. *Along the Gulf 1895*. W.A. White attorney at law published by the L&N Railroad, 1895.

French, Benjamin Franklin. *Historical Collections of Louisiana*. History of Louisiana from the memoir of Dumonte de Montigny

Husley, Val, and Edmond Boudreaux. *Historic Biloxi Queen of the Watering Holes*. Marceline, MO: Donning Company 2013.

Le Gac, Charles. *Immigration and War Louisiana 1718–1721, from the Memoir of Charles Le Gac*. Translated by Glenn R. Conrad. Lafayette: University of Southwest Louisiana, 1970.

McWilliams, Richebourg Gaillard. *Pierre Lemoyne d'Iberville Gulf Journals*. Tuscaloosa: University of Alabama Pres, 1981.

Remini, Robert V. *The Battle of New Orleans*. New York: Penguin Books, 2001.

Richmond, Stephanie C., and David Alfred Wheeler. *The Growth of the Biloxi Public School System*. Biloxi, MS: Biloxi Public Schools, 1979.

Scholtes, Collen C., and L.J. Scholtes. *Biloxi and the Mississippi Gulf Coast: A Pictorial History*. Norfolk, VA: Donning Co., 1985.

Suarez, Julie. *The Biloxi Cemetery*. Gulfport, MS: Mississippi Coast Historical and Genealogical Society, 2002.

Newspapers, Census, Directories, Magazine and Other Resources

Ancestry.com: "American Consular Service Certificate of Marriage for Harry Wendt and Julia Kipping, 1924." http://search.ancestry.com/search/db.aspx?dbid=1652.

———. "American Consular Service Deaths of Americans Abroad, 1835–1974." http://search.ancestry.com/search/db.aspx?dbid=1664.

———. "England and Wales Index of Wills and Administrations, 1861–1941." http://search.ancestry.com/search/db.aspx?dbid=8914.

———. "London, England, Marriages and Banns, 1754–1921." http://search.ancestry.com/search/db.aspx?dbid=8915.

———. "New Orleans City Directories, 1918–1950." http://search.ancestry.com/search/db.aspx?dbid=2469.

———. "Social Security Death Records." http://search.ancestry.com/search/db.aspx?dbid=3693.

———. "U.S. Passports, 1916–1945, for Harry Wendt and Julia Kipping Wendt." http://search.ancestry.com/search/db.aspx?dbid=1174.

———. "Wittenberg College Yearbook, 1916, Harry Wendt." http://search.ancestry.com/search/db.aspx?dbid=1265.

Baton Rouge (LA) Advocate. "Paul Prudhomme." August 3, 1978.

———. "Shrimp Tour Train." February 25, 1962.

———. "Six Gun Junction." August 30, 1964.

Bergeron, Kat. "Coast Chronicles: Biloxi USO Survives Only in Memory." *Biloxi (MS) Sun Herald*, August 21, 1994.

Biloxi Censuses, 1800–1949. Microfilm, United States Census Records, Historical and Genealogical Section, West Biloxi Public Library. Biloxi, MS: United States Census Bureau.

Biloxi (MS) Daily Herald. "A.B. Wood Dies Suddenly on Boat at Biloxi." May 1956.

———. "Biloxi's Handsome Hotel." December 28, 1923.

———. "Biloxi Shines." December 28, 1915.

———. "Biloxi's Oldest Library to Be Relocated, Restored." October 24, 1973.

———. "Crawford Taken by Death." May 29, 1915.

———. "The Creole Cottage." June 25, 1930.

———. "Dinty Moore." April 7, 1939.

———. "Dinty Moore's." April 16, 1937.

———. "Dr. Hunter." December 4, 1914.

———. "Eight Flags." May 1, 1971.
———. "Fire in Biloxi Friday Destroys Community Unit." August 20, 1966.
———. "Fisherman's Cottage." April 21, 1981.
———. "Golden Jubilee Number." Fiftieth Anniversary Souvenir edition, 1934.
———. "Gov. McLaurin." May 2, 1896.
———. "The Gulf View Hotel." April 7, 1888.
———. "Hospital Buys Eight Flags." February 2, 1985.
———. "Hotel Avelez." December 31, 1923.
———. "Hundreds Attend Opening Reception of Hotel Avelez." January 1, 1924.
———. "Ida Mae & Homer." April 30, 1928.
———. "Jessamine to Be Used in City Park." March 9, 1915.
———. "Latest City News." February 29, 1896.
———. "Memory of F.T. Howard Honored in Biloxi." October 24, 1911.
———. "Mrs. Pizzati." October 4, 1919.
———. "Park." March 13, 1901.
———. "Pavilion." March 17, 1915.
———. "Pavilion." June 19, 1915.
———. "Pavilion." October 12, 1915.
———. "Pavilion." June, 25, 1966.
———. "A Public Library." April 8, 1893.
———. "To the People of the Mississippi Coast." December 28, 1923.
———. "USO Begins New Activity in Biloxi." March 4, 1942.
———. "USO Building at Biloxi is Dedicated." March 16, 1942.
———. "USO Dedication Rites Set for First Night." March 11, 1942.
———. "USO Recreation Center in Biloxi to Open Monday." January 15, 1942.
———. "Work on the King's Daughters Library More Than One Thousand." March 23, 1911.
Biloxi (MS) Press. "Biloxi Water Cure." December 2, 1976.
Biloxi (MS) Sun Herald. "Baricev Obituaries." October 12, 1996.
———. "Baricev Obituary." August 25, 2011.
———. "Donald Jacobs Obituary." November 11, 2011.
———. "Father of Coast Tourism Dies at 85." November 9, 2011.
———. "Flashback Dinty Moore's & Friendship House." January 2, 1994.
———. "Log House Closing." August 25, 1998.
———. "Myerses Personify." October 14, 1984.
———. "You Can Almost Taste the Eggplant Josephine." June 24, 2012.

Boudreaux, Edmond. "History of Biloxi." City of Biloxi. http://www.biloxi.ms.us/visitor-info/history.

Brielmaier House file. Historical and Genealogical Section, West Biloxi Public Library, Biloxi, MS.

City of Biloxi Directories. 1907–1983. Historical and Genealogical Section, West Biloxi Public Library, Biloxi, MS.

"Cross Reference Gulf Coast Directories, 1993–1997." Gulf Coast Chamber of Commerce. Historical and Genealogical Section, West Biloxi Public Library, Biloxi, MS.

Down South. "A Gulf Coast Industry." November 1955.

Foretich House file. Community Development Department. City of Biloxi. Biloxi, MS.

Guice, Julia, and Annette O'Keefe. "Toledano History." Vertical Files. Historical and Genealogical Section, West Biloxi Public Library, Biloxi, MS.

Gus Stevens Seafood Restaurant and Lounge menu. Author's collection.

Harrison County. *Wills Harrison County Mississippi, 1853–1927*. Historical and Genealogical Section, West Biloxi Public Library, Biloxi, MS.

Harrison County Marriage Database. http://co.harrison.ms.us/elected/circuitclerk/marriage/judicial1.

Holt, Hazel. "Biloxi's Memorable Magnolia Hotel." *Down South*, April 1970.

Hotel Avelez. Stevens Collection. Vertical Files. Historical and Genealogical Section, West Biloxi Public Library, Biloxi, MS.

Jackson (MS) Clarion Ledger. "Creole Cottage." November 21, 1976.

James Steven's Collection. Historical and Genealogical Section, West Biloxi Public Library, Biloxi, MS.

Journal of Benjamin L. Wailes. 1852. Manuscript collection. Department of Archives and History, Jackson, MS.

Lund, Jim. "Landmark of 68 Years Victim of Time, Progress." *Gulfport (MS) Daily Herald*, March 18, 1965.

Magnolia Hotel Museum file. Vertical File. West Biloxi Library. Biloxi, MS.

Manor Papers. Historical and Genealogical Section, West Biloxi Public Library, Biloxi, MS.

Mobile (AL) Register. "Citizens." August 12, 1869.

Moon, Barbara. E-mails detailing purchase of L&N property by Nativity BVM. 2014.

Morris, Ted Allan. "A Short History of Operations at U.S. Coast Guard Air Station, Biloxi, Mississippi December 1934–March 1947." http://www.zianet.com/tmorris/biloxi.html.

Myers, Don. "Friendship House 1st Microwave." *Down South*. 1955.
———. "Log House." *Down South*. 1980.
New Orleans (LA) Times-Picayune. Advertisement, May 16, 1954.
———. "Baricev & Traina Marriage." October 11, 1925.
———. "Baricev Death." October 9, 1957.
———. "Big Gulf Hotel." August 2, 1925, sec. 2.
———. "Brennans Buy Friendship House." November 12, 1963.
———. "Chief of SBA Pleased on Coastal Area Tour." September 17, 1970.
———. "Coast Edgewater Gulf." July 26, 1971.
———. "Deer Ranch Ad." May 3, 1964.
———. "Dr. H.M. Folkes Dead." May 2, 1926.
———. "Edgewater Gulf Hotel." January 1, 1927.
———. "Edgewater Gulf Hotel." February 28, 1971, sec. 3.
———. "Eight Flags." May 7, 1972.
———. "Enjoy Fun, Sun on MS Gulf Coast." May 8, 1966, sec. 4.
———. "Friendship House." March 29, 1953.
———. "Friendship House." January 29, 1956.
———. "Friendship House." May 15, 1977.
———. "Gulf Coast Attractions." May 5, 1963.
———. "Gulf Coast Attractions." May 6, 1973.
———. "Hotel Operators on Coast." August 8, 1926, sec. 1.
———. "Many Visitors on Gulf Coast." January 16, 1927, sec. 2.
———. "Pizzati." November 3, 1903.
———. "Pizzati." December 31, 1915.
———. "Restaurant." May 27, 1934.
———. "Says New Hotel on Gulf Coast Opens Resort Era." September 7, 1925.
———. "Shrimp Train." May 7, 1961.
———. "Special Trains." October 17, 1926.
———. "Weatherman Aids Hotel." January 10, 1927.
New York Times. "Assassinated." October 29, 1893.
———. "A Noted Lottery Man Dead." June 1, 1885.
———. "Violating the Lottery Law." December 27, 1879.
Old Brick House file. Historical and Genealogical Section, West Biloxi Public Library, Biloxi, MS.
Old Tourist Rack Card on Father Ryan House. Historical and Genealogical Section, West Biloxi Public Library, Biloxi, MS.
Old Tourist Rack Card on Pleasant Reed House. Historical and Genealogical Section, West Biloxi Public Library, Biloxi, MS.

Pleasant Reed House files. Ohr-O'Keefe Museum of Art. Biloxi, MS.

Scholtes, Marguerite. "The White Pillars." *Down South*. 1970.

Stevens, Irene. Interview with the author. 2009.

St. Michaels Catholic Church. Vertical Files. Historical and Genealogical Section, West Biloxi Public Library, Biloxi, MS.

Telephone Directories. 1950–59. Historical and Genealogical Section, West Biloxi Public Library, Biloxi, MS.

Thompson, Ray M. "Baldwin Wood." Know Your State. *Biloxi (MS) Daily Herald*, June 22, 1961.

———. "Baldwin Wood." *New Orleans Magazine*, August 1972.

———. "Know Your State." *Biloxi (MS) Daily Herald*, August 13, 1956.

———. "The Little House That Isn't Here." Know Your Coast. *Biloxi (MS) Daily Herald*, 1957.

———. "The Man Who Made Water Flow Uphill." *Biloxi (MS) Daily Herald*, August 13, 1956.

———. "Palmer House." Know Your Coast. *Biloxi (MS) Daily Herald*, January 18, 1957.

Wesley House Folder. Vertical Files. Historical and Genealogical Section, West Biloxi Public Library, Biloxi, MS.

Index

A

American Riviera of the South 21

B

Bailey, Ada C. 11, 12
Bailey, Nathan Evans 11, 12
Baldwin Wood Lighthouse 127, 135
Barbay, Basilice Cleofas 69, 70
Baricev, Joseph P. 109, 110, 111, 112
Battle of New Orleans 70, 71
Beasley, Edwin King 120, 121
Beauregard, P.G.T. 129, 130
Beau Rivage Casino and Resort 112, 116
Biloxi Coast Guard Air Station 150, 151, 153
Biloxi Garden Club 52
Biloxi Library 22, 24, 25
Biloxi Lighthouse Visitor Center 30
Biloxi Shrimp Tour Train 156, 157, 158, 160
Biloxi Town Green 16, 19, 20
Biloxi Yacht Club 95, 117
Boggs, George H. 153
Boullemet, Maria Palmira 127, 128, 129, 130
Boykin, Minnie 12
Brennan family 124
Brielmaier, Paul W. 16, 17, 18
Buccaneer Lounge. *See* Gus Stevens Restaurant and Supper Club
Buena Vista Hotel 78, 94, 102, 107, 112, 116, 117
Byrenheidt, Andreas 76, 77

C

Caldwell, Phil C. 86, 88, 89
Captain Plauche's battalion 71
Carquotte, Jean Baptiste 51
City of Biloxi tricentennial 30
Civil War 33, 41, 42, 51, 96, 105, 106

Creole Cottage 21, 24, 25
Curet, Mary Adrienne 14, 15

D

Dantzler, A.F. 28
Davis, Jefferson 35
de Bienville, Jean Baptiste Lemoyne 48
Delauney, John 21, 58
Dewey, William M. 84

E

Early, Jubal A. 129
Eight Flags Deer Ranch 124, 156, 157, 158, 160
Enoch, Cora Inez 96, 97, 98, 99, 101

F

Fairchild, Jack 122
Folkes, Hyman McMackin 60, 61, 62
Fountain, Martin 38
French Restaurant 111

G

Gollott, Tommy 38
Gulf View Hotel 77, 78
Gus Stevens Café and Bar 116
Gus Stevens Restaurant and Supper Club 113, 114, 115, 116, 118, 119

H

Hahn, Elizabeth 105, 106
Hahn, John 103, 104, 105
Harkness, John R. and G.A. 142
Harrison, Pat 150
Henley, John L. 51, 52
Holy Angels Nursery 11, 14, 15, 59
Howard, Annie Turner 127, 128, 129, 132
Howard, Charles Turner 127, 128, 129, 130
Howard, Frank Turner 127, 128, 129, 130, 132, 133
Howard, Harry Turner 22, 127, 128, 129, 130, 131, 132
Hurricane Camille 14, 15, 28, 30, 53, 67, 75, 76, 79, 107, 112, 127, 130, 135
Hurricane Katrina 15, 16, 17, 20, 21, 25, 26, 30, 31, 37, 38, 40, 41, 45, 46, 51, 53, 55, 59, 72, 75, 91, 95, 103, 108, 133, 150, 154, 155, 161

J

Jacobs, Donald "Don" Patrick 156, 157, 158, 160, 161

K

Kipping, Julia 63
Kouvarakis, Constantine Gus Stamatios. *See* Gus Stevens

L

Le Blanc, M. 49
Le Gac, Charles 48
Log House 124, 125, 126
Lopez, Theresa 60, 61, 62, 63
Louisiana state lottery 129, 130

M

Maloney, James M. 28
Mansfield, Jayne 118
Mardi Gras Museum 30, 108
Marine Life Oceanarium 156, 158, 160, 161
Maritime and Seafood Industry Museum 135, 150, 151, 154, 155
Marshall, Benjamin H. 80
Martin, Homer 120
Memphis Hotel 78, 79
Milner, Earle Reid 90
Mississippi Alumni Chapter of Delta Sigma Theta Sorority, Inc. 44
Mitchell, Irene 116, 117
Mladinich, Jake, Jr. 66, 67
Mladinich, Jake, Sr. 66, 67
Mladinich, John M. 68
mud daub house 47, 48, 49, 50
Myers, Jim 121, 122, 123, 124, 126

N

Nativity of the Blessed Virgin Mary Church 13, 61, 146, 148
Notre Dame High School 28
Nydia 133, 134, 135

O

Ohr-O'Keefe Museum of Art 41, 44, 45, 46
O'Keefe, Jerry 38, 40
O'Keefe, John 35

P

Palmer, Charles 78, 79
Parrish, Mary Anderson 122
Peirotich, Mary 66
Philippines 63, 64, 65
Pizzati, Salvadore 146, 147, 148
Plauche's Battalion d'Orleans 69, 70
Poet Laureate of the South 33
Pradat, Mathilde 69, 70, 71, 72, 73

R

Reed family 41, 42, 44, 45
Reed, Walter 62
Robinson, John Ghamm 26, 27
Rodenberg, Millie 23
Rosell, T.J. 99
Rue Magnolia 25, 56, 108
Ryan, Father Abram J. 33, 34, 35, 37

S

Sacred Heart Academy 28, 148
Santo Tomas University, Manila 63, 64
Sicuro, Salvatore and Josephine 90
Six Gun Junction 124, 156, 158, 160
Stevens, Gus 113, 114, 116, 117, 118, 119
St. Michael's Church 14

T

Toledano, Christoval Sebastian 69, 70, 71, 73
Trade Winds Hotel 94, 95
Traina, Jessie 109, 112
Tullis, Garner 73, 74

V

Valenzano, Francesco "Frances" 146, 148

W

Wade, W.C. 31
Wailes, Benjamin L. 76
War of 1812 69, 71
Wendt, Harry Alden 63, 64
Wendt, Julia 65
Wesley House 11, 13
White, Cora. *See* Cora Inez Enoch
White, H. 153
White, Walter A. 96, 97, 98, 101, 102
Wood, Albert Baldwin 130, 132, 133, 134, 135

About the Author

Edmond Boudreaux was born in 1949 to Edmond Boudreaux Sr. and Nita Mae Thomas. He is a 1967 graduate of Notre Dame High School in Biloxi, Mississippi. He is married to Virginia L. Bertucci, and they have three sons: Edmond III, married to Christy Cranston; Brandon, husband of Heather Swetman; and Marcus, married to Michelle Wagner. Edmond and Virginia have nine grandchildren. He is the administrative vice-president of the Mississippi Coast Historical and Genealogical Society, past president of the Gulf Coast chapter of the Mississippi Archaeological Association, an acquisition committee member of the Ohr-O'Keefe Museum of Art, an advisory board member of the Maritime and Seafood Industry Museum, a member of the community advisory committee at the Mississippi State Historical Museum and a French colonial reenactor since 1992. He is author of the "Time Traveler" article series for the *Biloxi/D'Iberville Press* newspaper. He was awarded the Calvin Brown Award and the Mississippi Governor Commendation for archaeology in 1992, as well as being named city of Biloxi's Historian of the Year in 1993. In 2011, the Mississippi Department of Archives and History (MDAH) presented him with a Resolution of Commendation for his leadership in historical causes, his work in support of MDAH programs and his scholarship on the history of the Gulf Coast. He is co-author with Val Husley, PhD, of *Historic Biloxi: Queen of the Watering Holes* (2013), published by the Donning Company. He is the author of *The Seafood Capital of the World: Biloxi's Maritime History* (2011) and *Legend and Lore of the Mississippi Golden Gulf Coast* (2013), both published by The History Press.

Visit us at
www.historypress.net

This title is also available as an e-book

CPSIA information can be obtained
at www.ICGtesting.com
Printed in the USA
LVHW080443140222
711067LV00004B/107